1143009918971
12.4 Endocrine
he endocrine system /

Main

THE ENDOCRINE SYSTEM

THE HUMAN BODY

THE ENDOCRINE SYSTEM

EDITED BY KARA ROGERS, SENIOR EDITOR, BIOMEDICAL SCIENCES

Britannica
Educational Publishing

IN ASSOCIATION WITH

ROSEN
EDUCATIONAL SERVICES

Published in 2012 by Britannica Educational Publishing
(a trademark of Encyclopædia Britannica, Inc.)
in association with Rosen Educational Services, LLC
29 East 21st Street, New York, NY 10010.

First Edition

Britannica Educational Publishing
Michael I. Levy: Executive Editor
J.E. Luebering: Senior Manager
Adam Augustyn: Assistant Manager
Marilyn L. Barton: Senior Coordinator, Production Control
Steven Bosco: Director, Editorial Technologies
Lisa S. Braucher: Senior Producer and Data Editor
Yvette Charboneau: Senior Copy Editor
Kathy Nakamura: Manager, Media Acquisition
Kara Rogers: Senior Editor, Biomedical Sciences

Rosen Educational Services
Alexandra Hanson-Harding: Editor
Hope Lourie Killcoyne: Executive Editor
Nelson Sá: Art Director
Cindy Reiman: Photography Manager
Karen Huang: Photo Researcher
Matthew Cauli: Designer, Cover Design
Introduction by Jennifer Capuzzo

Library of Congress Cataloging-in-Publication Data

The endocrine system/edited by Kara Rogers.—1st ed.
   p. cm.—(The human body)
"In association with Britannica Educational Publishing, Rosen Educational Services."
Includes bibliographical references and index.
ISBN 978-1-61530-675-6 (lib. bdg.)
   1. Endocrine glands—Physiology—Juvenile literature. 2. Endocrine glands—Diseases—
Juvenile literature. I. Rogers, Kara.
QP187.E6937 2012
612.4—dc23

                                                                      2011032611

Manufactured in the United States of America

On the cover: The endocrine system is comprised of hormone-producing glands. Major
endocrine glands include the pituitary, thyroid, and adrenal glands, as well as the pancreas.
Additionally, women have ovaries and men have testes. *MedicalRF.com/Getty Images*

On page xii: A woman having her thyroid gland examined by ultrasound. From hyperthyroidism
(excess production of thyroid hormone by the thyroid gland) to hypothyroidism (a deficiency of
the hormone), women are more likely than men to suffer from thyroid conditions. *Shutterstock.com*

On pages 1, 32, 63, 102, 132, 155, 180, 197, 199, 203, 205: Thyroxine is one of the two major
hormones secreted by the thyroid gland (the other is triiodothyronine). Thyroxine's principal
function is to stimulate oxygen consumption and thus the metabolism of all cells and tissues in
the body. © *www.istockphoto.com/Shunyu Fan*

CONTENTS

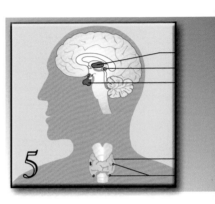

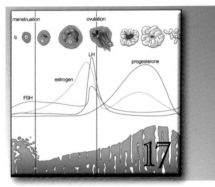

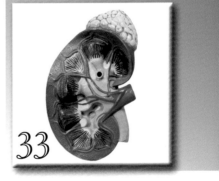

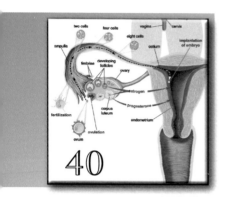

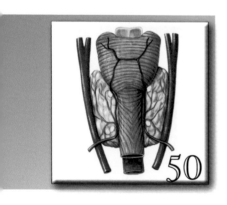

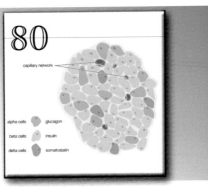

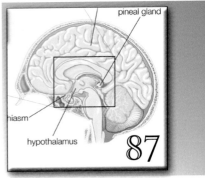

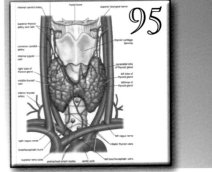

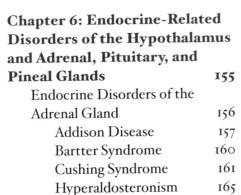

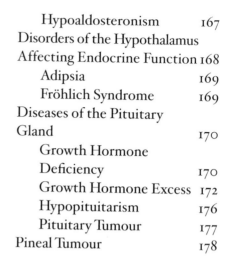

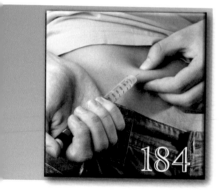

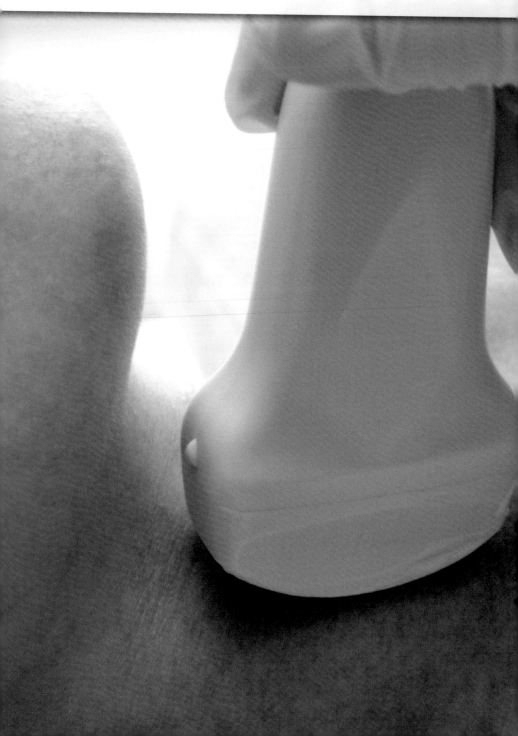

INTRODUCTION

As a person matures from an infant into an adult, the seemingly simple progression of growth and development is directed by the stunningly complex endocrine system. Precise levels of hormones, cellular fluids, and metabolic chemicals need to be maintained for a person to lead a healthy life. In order to meet those needs, the endocrine system constantly regulates the activities of organs and tissues.

Endocrine glands secrete hormones into the bloodstream, targeting specific organs and tissues. Collectively, these glands make up the endocrine system and include but are not limited to the pituitary, thyroid, pancreas, ovaries, and testes. Self-regulation helps the system maintain order and stability among the body's organs, but factors that compromise the balance in the system, such as tumours, result in illness.

Four principle components support endocrine function: the endocrine gland, the hormone it secretes, the tissue targeted by the secreted hormone, and the response of that tissue to the hormone. The glands themselves consist of specialized cells and a large number of blood vessels that help deliver nutrients to the glands. The blood vessels play an important role in the system, primarily because they carry hormones from one place to another.

The two main types of hormones are protein hormones, which include peptides and amino acids, and steroid hormones, which are synthesized from cholesterol. Steroid hormones move through the bloodstream as free hormones and as hormones bound to specific proteins. The free hormones target tissues and exert hormonal activity. Protein hormones, on the other hand, are initially contained with inactive molecules known as prohormones. After an enzyme splits the prohormone, the active portion of the hormone separates from the inactive molecule and travels from the cell into the blood.

Hormones bind to and activate receptor molecules, which are found either on the surface of a target cell or within the cell's cytoplasm or nucleus. Each hormone affects only those tissues containing receptors designed for that specific hormone. The activation of a receptor initiates a specific chemical response; for example, hormone-receptor binding may lead to the activation of a particular enzyme, to the stimulation of protein synthesis, or to the secretion of another hormone.

The endocrine system regulates itself in a precise and intricate manner. In general, an endocrine gland secretes more or less of its hormone depending on the concentration in the blood of a substance such as another hormone or a nutrient. The simplest way endocrine glands regulate themselves is through a negative feedback mechanism. When the endocrine glands themselves are the target organs, however, the process of self-regulation is more complex and involves interconnecting negative feedback loops. Additional control mechanisms include paracrine control and autocrine control. In paracrine control, if an endocrine gland is made up of different types of cells, one cell type can secrete hormones that impact a different cell type. Hence, different cell types work together to regulate hormone secretions within that one gland. Autocrine control occurs when the same cell type affects its own activity. In either case, both of these supplemental mechanisms are examples of how endocrine cell activity can be controlled from within the gland itself.

A major function of the endocrine system is to provide homeostasis, a vital mechanism that facilitates body activities and simultaneously maintains a constant balance of cellular body fluids. The concentration of various salts, or electrolytes, in the body fluids needs to remain constant. Changes in the circulating blood's electrolyte concentration trigger the endocrine system to restore order through negative feedback regulatory mechanisms.

An increase in electrolytes outside the cells prompts the movement of intracellular fluid across the cell membrane and into the extracellular fluid, resulting in dehydration. A decrease in the concentration of electrolytes outside the cells results in excess fluid within the cells. Homeostasis keeps the levels of electrolytes constant, helping the body avoid potential problems. Additionally, homeostasis also maintains healthy levels of plasma volume and nutrients necessary for body metabolism.

The endocrine system not only helps maintain a constant internal environment, but it also controls the growth and development of the organism. Precisely timed hormonal changes control the impact that maturation, aging, and sexual differentiation have on the body's internal environment. The endocrine system initiates and controls the transformation of an adolescent into an adult.

Stressful internal and external stimuli also impact the endocrine system's hormonal secretions. "Fight-or-flight" responses in animals include increased secretion of cortisol by the adrenal cortex, increased secretion of glucagon by the pancreas, and increased secretion of epinephrine and norepinephrine by the adrenal medulla. More prolonged stresses, such as starvation or malnutrition, affect production of thyroid hormone, lowering the metabolic rate. This mechanism slows the consumption of the body's fuel and energy stores, deferring death from starvation.

In order for these vital responses to take place, the body must synthesize and transport hormones. A metabolite stimulates protein hormone synthesis when it enters a target cell's cytoplasm or nucleus. The protein hormone binds to a receptor on the cell's surface, initiating a complex series of events within the cell that activate specific genes that direct the synthesis of a target cell's prohormone. As the prohormone travels to the cell surface, the hormone is cleaved from the prohormone.

Most hormones are secreted into the general circulation and exist as either unbound hormones or as hormones bound to a transport protein. Protein-bound hormones are in equilibrium with a concentration of unbound hormones in serum. As the free hormones exit circulation and target their specific tissues, bound hormones break free from their binding proteins to maintain balance in the serum. Feedback mechanisms help maintain circulating hormone balance.

After introducing the human endocrine system and its function and regulation, this volume explains the role that specific endocrine hormones play in the body's growth and metabolism. The pituitary gland, for example, releases adrenocorticotropin (ACTH), growth hormone (GH), and thryotropin (thyroid stimulating hormone), among other hormones, to stimulate the growth and development of different systems within the body. Other glands such as the testes and ovaries stimulate the development of sex organs and secondary sex characteristics.

Experts have created select tests to evaluate the function of specific endocrine glands. The epinephrine tolerance test evaluates the body's ability to metabolize the storage form of glucose. The protein-bound iodine test evaluates thyroid function by measuring the concentration of iodine bound to proteins in the bloodstream. This indirect test has been replaced by the more direct thyroid function test. The newer test measures the concentration of thyrotropin and thyroxine (a hormone secreted by the thyroid gland) in the blood. A person with an overactive thyroid gland has high serum thyroid hormone and low serum thyrotropin concentrations. Conversely, a person with an underactive thyroid has low serum thyroid and high serum thyrotropin concentrations.

In some cases, endocrine hypofunction, which manifests as a decrease in hormone production, is a necessary step in maintaining homeostasis. During starvation and illness, for example, thyroid hormones need to be at a low concentration in order to slow the body's metabolism, since food intake is low. This survival mechanism is an example of compensatory endocrine hypofunction. Another example of an acquired cause of endocrine hypofunction is surgery. If one of a paired gland is removed, the remaining gland may increase in size and activity to sustain normal hormone levels. Bacterial, fungal, and viral infections, among other factors, can also cause acquired endocrine hypofunction.

Congenital (birth) defects can cause endocrine gland hypofunction. Drugs and other substances absorbed through the placenta during fetal development can block hormone production or stunt the growth and formation of an endocrine gland. Genetic mutations can cause deficient enzyme production necessary for hormone synthesis. Most commonly, however, endocrine hypofunction is a result of autoimmunity. In such cases, immune cells erroneously produce antibodies that react with the body's tissue cells rather than with foreign substances. This action alters an endocrine gland's function by killing the gland's cells, blocking the binding of hormones to their receptors, or stimulating or inhibiting the normal hormonal balance.

Other causes of endocrine hypofunction include changes in biochemical environments. Dietary concerns and drugs can impact the biochemical environment and inhibit hormone production. A diet lacking adequate iodine, for example, causes a decrease in available thyroid hormone. Furthermore, lithium, a drug used to treat the neurobiological condition known as bipolar disorder, blocks thyroid hormone synthesis.

An abnormality within an endocrine gland or changes in the level of a hormone-regulating substance in the blood can cause endocrine hyperfunction. In the case of hyperfunction, some glands become hypertrophic (when the size of each cell in the affected gland increases), and some glands become hyperplastic (when the number of cells in those glands increases). Some of the cells of a hyperplastic gland can result in the formation of a tumour. Most endocrine tumours are benign (noncancerous). Other tumours, however, may be malignant (cancerous). In such instances, the cancer not only may cause endocrine hyperfunction but also may be capable of spreading to distant organs. Some tumours arise from tissues that typically have no endocrine function but suddenly begin producing one or more hormones. Such tumours are known as ectopic hormone-producing tumours. As an example, certain forms of lung cancer have been known to produce antidiuretic hormone (also known as vasopressin).

Although years ago scientists subscribed to an "endocrine theory of aging," many experts now agree that growing older has relatively minor affects on endocrine function. The changes that do occur generally pose little threat to an aging person's daily activities. Thyroid and adrenal functions, for example, do not significantly change with age. In fact, the slight decrease of aldosterone, a steroid hormone secreted by the adrenal glands to maintain healthy salt and water balance, has little effect on the body. As such, elderly people are able to maintain normal fluid and electrolyte balance. Growth hormone secretion, bone mass and density, and production of testosterone in men and estrogen in women all decrease as a result of aging.

After detailing the nature of endocrine dysfunction, this volume will investigate the diseases and disorders of various secretory glands. Graves disease, for example, is the most common cause of hyperthyroidism. As a result of excessive thyroid hormone secretion, the thyroid gland is abnormally enlarged, a condition known as diffuse goitre. While there is no treatment for Graves disease, hyperthyroidism can be treated with an antithyroid drug or radioactive iodine. In few cases, removal of the thyroid may be necessary.

Diseases and disorders of the pituitary gland include growth hormone deficiency and growth hormone excess.

Growth hormone deficiency causes dwarfism and short stature and often results from damage to the pituitary gland during fetal development or following birth. Children who suffer from growth hormone deficiency do not show signs of growth retardation at birth, but X-rays of the growing ends of bones can reveal effects of the disease within the first two years of life. Growth hormone excess, on the other hand, is usually caused by a benign tumour of the pituitary gland. When these tumours occur in children, they can cause excessive height, or gigantism, and enlargement of body parts, also known as acromegaly. Treatment for this type of disorder includes surgery of the pituitary tumour, radiation therapy, or drugs that inhibit the secretion of growth hormone.

Disorders of the endocrine pancreas affect glucose metabolism. The pancreas contains patches of endocrine tissue known as the islets of Langerhans that produce insulin. Growth hormone and glucagon trigger the production of insulin, promoting the metabolism of glucose and preventing the release of glucose by the liver. Increased concentrations of glucose in the blood stimulate the release of insulin from the pancreas. Insulin counteracts the increased glucose levels. This homeostatic relationship is compromised when the islet cells cannot make sufficient amounts of insulin to control blood glucose levels. This disorder is known as diabetes mellitus. Pancreatic cancer can also affect the function of the islets of Langerhans.

Just as a tiny grain of sand can cause major mechanical failure in a finely tuned machine, so too can the endocrine system fall victim to the slightest change in internal or external environment. Its self-regulating capabilities can counter some biophysical alterations, but the necessary balance of hormones, bodily fluids, and metabolic chemicals is a sensitive science, one that the endocrine system constantly tries to maintain.

CHAPTER 1

FUNCTION AND REGULATION OF THE HUMAN ENDOCRINE SYSTEM

The human endocrine system consists of a group of ductless glands that regulate body processes by secreting chemical substances called hormones. Hormones act on nearby tissues or are carried in the bloodstream to act on specific target organs and distant tissues.

It is important to distinguish between an endocrine gland, which discharges hormones into the bloodstream, and an exocrine gland, which secretes substances through a duct opening in a gland onto an external or internal body surface. Salivary glands and sweat glands are examples of exocrine glands. Both saliva, secreted by the salivary glands, and sweat, secreted by the sweat glands, act on local tissues near the duct openings. In contrast, the hormones secreted by endocrine glands are carried by the circulation to exert their actions on tissues remote from the site of their secretion.

As far back as 3000 BCE, the ancient Chinese were able to diagnose and provide effective treatments for some endocrinologic disorders. For example, seaweed, which is rich in iodine, was prescribed for the treatment of goitre (enlargement of the thyroid gland). Perhaps the earliest demonstration of direct endocrinologic intervention in humans was the castration of men who could then be relied upon, more or less, to safeguard the chastity of women living in harems. During the Middle Ages and later, the practice persisting well into the 19th century, prepubertal boys were sometimes castrated to preserve the purity of their treble voices. Castration established the testes (testicles) as the source of substances responsible for the development and maintenance of "maleness."

This knowledge led to an abiding interest in restoring or enhancing male sexual powers. In the 18th century, London-based Scottish surgeon, anatomist, and physiologist John Hunter successfully transplanted the testis of a rooster into the abdomen of a hen. In the 19th century, French neurologist and physiologist Charles-Édouard Brown-Séquard asserted that the testes contained an invigorating, rejuvenating substance. His conclusions were based in part on observations obtained after he had injected himself with an extract of the testicle of a dog or of a guinea pig. These experiments resulted in the widespread use of organ extracts to treat endocrine conditions (organotherapy).

Modern endocrinology largely developed in the 20th century. Its scientific origin is rooted in the studies of French physiologist Claude Bernard (1813–78), who made the key observation that complex organisms such as humans go to great lengths to preserve the constancy of what he called the "milieu intérieur" (internal environment). Later, American physiologist Walter Bradford Cannon (1871–1945) used the term *homeostasis* to describe this inner constancy.

The endocrine system, in association with the nervous system and the immune system, regulates the body's internal activities and the body's interactions with the external environment to preserve the internal environment. This control system permits the prime functions of living organisms — growth, development, and reproduction — to proceed in an orderly, stable fashion. It is exquisitely self-regulating, so that any disruption of the normal internal environment by internal or external events is resisted by powerful countermeasures. When this resistance is overcome, illness ensues. In general, diseases of the endocrine system result from the oversecretion or undersecretion of hormones or from the inability of target organs or tissues to respond to hormones effectively.

The body of knowledge of the endocrine system is continually expanding, driven in large part by research that seeks to understand basic cell functions and basic mechanisms of human endocrine diseases and disorders. The traditional core of an endocrine system consists of an endocrine gland, the hormone it secretes, a responding tissue containing a specific receptor to which the hormone binds, and an action that results after the hormone binds to its receptor (the postreceptor response).

Each endocrine gland consists of a group of specialized cells that have a common origin in the developing embryo. Some endocrine glands, such as the thyroid gland in the lower neck, below the voice box (or larynx), and the islets of Langerhans in the pancreas, are derived from cells that arise in the embryonic digestive system. Other endocrine glands, such as the parathyroid glands, also in the lower neck, and the adrenal medulla, found in the centre of the cortex of the adrenal glands, which are located above the kidneys, are derived from cells that arise in the embryonic nervous system. Certain glands, including the ovary, testis, and adrenal cortex, arise from a region of the embryo known as the urogenital ridge. There are also several glands that are derived from cells that originate in multiple regions of the embryo. For example, the pituitary gland is composed of cells from the nervous system and the digestive tract.

Each endocrine gland also has a rich supply of blood vessels. This is important not only because nutrients are delivered to the gland by the blood vessels but also because the gland cells that line these vessels are able to detect serum levels of specific hormones or other substances that directly effect the synthesis and secretion of the hormone the gland produces. Serum is the watery portion of plasma—the fluid part of blood—that remains after other parts coagulate. Hormone secretion is sometimes very complex, because many endocrine glands secrete more than one hormone. In addition, some organs function both as exocrine glands and as endocrine glands. The best-known example of such an organ is the pancreas.

In addition to traditional endocrine cells, specially modified nerve cells within the nervous system secrete important hormones into the blood. These special nerve cells are called neurosecretory cells, and their secretions are known as neurohormones to distinguish them from the hormones produced by traditional endocrine cells. Neurohormones are stored in the terminals of neurosecretory cells and are released into the bloodstream upon stimulation of the cells.

Most hormones are one of two types: protein hormones, including peptides—substances in which the molecules are structurally like proteins, but smaller—or steroid hormones. The majority of hormones are protein hormones. They are highly soluble in water and can be transported readily through the blood. When initially synthesized within the cell, protein hormones are contained within large biologically inactive molecules called prohormones. An enzyme splits the inactive portion from the active portion of the prohormone, thereby forming the active hormone that is then released from the cell into the blood. There are fewer steroid hormones than protein hormones, and all steroid hormones are synthesized from the precursor molecule cholesterol. These hormones (and a few of the protein hormones) circulate in the blood both as hormone that is free and as hormone that is bound to specific proteins. It is the free unbound hormone that has access to tissues to exert hormonal activity.

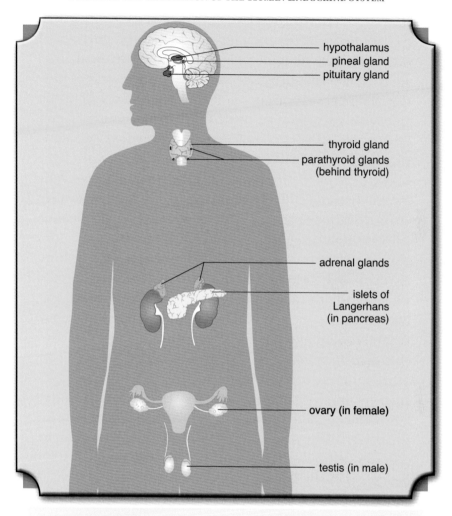

Major glands of the human endocrine system. The hypothalamus stimulates the pituitary gland and influences food intake, weight regulation, fluid intake and balance, thirst, body heat, and the sleep cycle. Pituitary hormones stimulate growth, egg and sperm development, milk secretion, and release of hormones by other glands. The pineal gland may play a significant role in sexual maturation and the circadian rhythm. Thyroid hormones regulate the metabolic rate of tissues, stimulate the contraction of heart muscle, and are necessary for normal growth and brain development before birth and during infancy. Parathyroid hormone regulates calcium, phosphorus, and magnesium levels. The adrenal glands regulate salt and water retention, some reactions of the immune system, and blood pressure. The islets of Langerhans regulate blood sugar levels. The ovaries and testes produce hormones that regulate the reproductive system and that produce male and female secondary sex characteristics. © Merriam-Webster Inc.

Hormones act on their target tissues by binding to and activating specific molecules called receptors. Receptors are found on the surface of target cells in the case of protein and peptide hormones, or they are found within the cytoplasm (a substance made up of water, proteins, and other molecules surrounded by a membrane) or nuclei (the organelle housing a cell's genetic material) of target cells in the case of steroid hormones and thyroid hormones. Each receptor has a strong, highly specific affinity (attraction) for a particular hormone. A hormone can have an effect only on those tissues that contain receptors specific for that hormone. Often, one segment of the hormone molecule has a strong chemical affinity for the receptor while another segment is responsible for initiating the hormone's specific action. Thus, hormonal actions are not general throughout the body but rather are aimed at specific target tissues.

A hormone-receptor complex activates a chain of specific chemical responses within the cells of the target tissue to complete hormonal action. This action may be the result of the activation of enzymes within the target cell, interaction of the hormone-receptor complex with the deoxyribonucleic acid (DNA) in the nucleus of the cell (and consequent stimulation of protein synthesis), or a combination of both. It may even result in the secretion of another hormone.

THE NATURE OF ENDOCRINE REGULATION

Endocrine gland secretion is not a haphazard process. It is subject to precise, intricate control so that its effects may be integrated with those of the nervous system and the immune system. The simplest level of control over endocrine gland secretion resides at the endocrine gland itself.

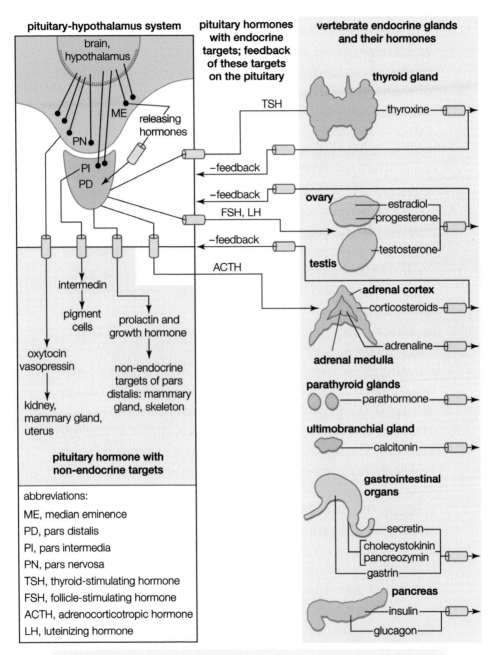

The pituitary gland secretes multiple hormones, including melanocyte-stimulating hormone (MSH, or intermedin), adrenocorticotropic hormone (ACTH), and thyrotropin (thyroid-stimulating hormone, or TSH).
Encyclopædia Britannica, Inc.

The signal for an endocrine gland to secrete more or less of its hormone is related to the concentration of some substance, either a hormone that influences the function of the gland (a tropic hormone), a biochemical product (e.g., glucose), or a biologically important element (e.g., calcium or potassium). Because each endocrine gland has a rich supply of blood, each gland is able to detect small changes in the concentrations of its regulating substances.

Some endocrine glands are controlled by a simple negative feedback mechanism. (Feedback mechanisms are discussed later in this chapter.) For example, negative feedback signaling mechanisms in the parathyroid glands rely on the binding activity of calcium-sensitive receptors that are located on the surface of parathyroid cells. Decreased serum calcium concentrations result in decreased calcium receptor binding activity that stimulates the secretion of parathormone from the parathyroid glands. The increased serum concentration of parathormone stimulates bone resorption (breakdown) to release calcium into the blood and reabsorption of calcium in the kidney to retain calcium in the blood, thereby restoring serum calcium concentrations to normal levels. In contrast, increased serum calcium concentrations result in increased calcium receptor-binding activity and inhibition of parathormone secretion by the parathyroid glands. This allows serum calcium concentrations to decrease to normal levels. Therefore, in people with normal parathyroid glands, serum calcium concentrations are maintained within a very narrow range even in the presence of large changes in calcium intake or excessive losses of calcium from the body.

Control of the hormonal secretions of other endocrine glands is more complex, because the glands themselves are target organs of a regulatory system called the hypothalamic-pituitary-target gland axis. The major mechanisms in this regulatory system consist of complex interconnecting negative feedback loops that involve the hypothalamus (a structure located at the base of the brain and above the pituitary gland), the anterior pituitary gland, and the target gland. The hypothalamus produces specific neurohormones that stimulate the pituitary gland to secrete specific pituitary hormones that affect any of a number of target organs, including the adrenal cortex, the gonads (testes and ovaries), and the thyroid gland. Therefore, the hypothalamic-pituitary-target gland axis allows for both neural and hormonal input into hormone production by the target gland.

When stimulated by the appropriate pituitary hormone, the target gland secretes its hormone (target gland hormone) that then combines with receptors located on its target tissues. These receptors include receptors located on the pituitary cells that make the particular hormone that governs the target gland. Should the amount of target gland hormone in the blood increase, the hormone's actions on its target organs increases. In the pituitary gland, the target gland hormone acts to decrease the secretion of the appropriate pituitary hormone, which results in less stimulation of the target gland and a decrease in the production of hormone by the target gland. Conversely, if hormone production by a target gland should decrease, the decrease in serum concentrations of the target gland hormone leads to an increase in secretion of the pituitary hormone in an attempt to restore target gland hormone production to normal. The effect of the target gland hormone on its target tissues is quantitative—within limits, the greater (or lesser) the amount of target gland hormone bound to receptors in the target tissues, the greater (or lesser) the response of the target tissues.

In the hypothalamic-pituitary-target gland axis, a second negative feedback loop is superimposed on the first negative feedback loop. In this second loop, the target gland hormone binds to nerve cells in the hypothalamus, thereby inhibiting the secretion of specific hypothalamic-releasing hormones (neurohormones) that stimulate the secretion of pituitary hormones (an important element in the first negative feedback loop). The hypothalamic neurohormones are released within a set of veins that connects the hypothalamus to the pituitary gland (the hypophyseal-portal circulation), and therefore the neurohormones reach the pituitary gland in high concentrations. Target gland hormones effect the secretion of hypothalamic hormones in the same way that they effect the secretion of pituitary hormones, thereby reinforcing their effect on the production of the pituitary hormone.

The importance of the second negative feedback loop lies in the fact that the nerve cells of the hypothalamus receive impulses from other regions of the brain, including the cerebral cortex (the centre for higher mental function, movement, perception, emotion, etc.), thus permitting the endocrine system to respond to physical and emotional stresses. This response mechanism involves the interruption of the primary feedback loop to allow the serum concentrations of hormones to be increased or decreased in response to environmental stresses that activate the nervous system. The end result of the two negative feedback loops is that, under ordinary circumstances, hormone production by target glands and the serum concentrations of target gland hormone are maintained within very narrow limits but that, under extraordinary circumstances, this tight control can be overridden by stimuli originating outside of the endocrine system.

There are important supplemental mechanisms that control endocrine function. When more than one cell type is found within a single endocrine gland, the hormones secreted by one cell type may exert a direct modulating effect upon the secretions of the other cell types. This form of control is known as paracrine control. Similarly, the secretions of one endocrine cell may alter the activity of the same cell, an activity known as autocrine control. Thus, endocrine cell activity may be modulated directly from within the endocrine gland itself, without the need for hormones to enter the bloodstream.

If the requirement that a hormone act at a site remote from the endocrine cells in which the hormone is produced is excluded from the defining characteristics of hormones, additional classes of biologically active materials can be considered as hormones. Neurotransmitters, a group of chemical compounds of variable composition, are secreted at all synapses (junctions between nerve cells over which nervous impulses must travel). They facilitate or inhibit the transmission of neural impulses and have given rise to the science of neuroendocrinology (the branch of medicine that studies the interaction of the nervous system and the endocrine system). A second group of biologically active substances is called prostaglandins. Prostaglandins are a complex group of fatty acid derivatives that are produced and secreted by many tissues. Prostaglandins mediate important biological effects in almost every organ system of the body.

Another group of substances, called growth factors, possess hormonelike activity. Growth factors are substances that stimulate the growth of specific tissues. They are distinct from pituitary growth hormone in that they were identified only after it was noted that target cells grown outside the organism in tissue culture could be stimulated to grow and reproduce by extracts of serum or tissue chemically distinct from growth hormone.

Still another area of hormonal activity that has come under intensive investigation is the effect of endocrine hormones on behaviour. While simple direct hormonal effects on human behaviour are difficult to document because of the complexities of human motivation, there are many convincing demonstrations of hormone-mediated behaviour in other life-forms. A special case is that of the pheromone, a substance generated by an organism that influences, by its odour, the behaviour of another organism of the same species. An often-quoted example is the musky scent of the females of many species, which provokes sexual excitation in the male. Such mechanisms have adaptive value for species survival.

THE ENDOCRINE SYSTEM AND THE HUMAN SYSTEM

The endocrine system, consisting of many different glands, hormones, and target tissues, governs a variety of physiological processes. Among the most important of these are its roles in maintaining tissue health, regulating tissue growth, guiding stress response, prompting parenting behaviours, and integrating gland and hormone activity following injury or illness.

MAINTENANCE OF HOMEOSTASIS

For an organism to function normally and effectively, it is necessary that the biochemical processes of its tissues operate smoothly and conjointly in a stable setting. The endocrine system provides the essential mechanism called homeostasis that integrates body activities and at the same time ensures that the composition of the body fluids bathing the constituent cells remains constant.

Scientists have postulated that the concentrations of the various salts present in the fluids of the body closely resemble the concentrations of salts in the primordial seas, which nourished the simple organisms from which increasingly complex species have evolved. Any change in the salt composition of fluids that surround cells, such as the extracellular fluid and the fluid portion of the circulating blood (the serum), necessitates large compensating changes in the salt concentrations within cells. As a result, the constancy of these salts (electrolytes) inside and outside of cells is closely guarded. Even small changes in the serum concentrations of these electrolytes (e.g., sodium, potassium, chloride, calcium, magnesium, and phosphate) elicit prompt responses from the endocrine system in order to restore normal concentrations. These responses are initiated through negative feedback regulatory mechanisms similar to those described previously.

Not only is the concentration of each individual electrolyte maintained through homeostasis, but the total concentration of all of the electrolytes per unit of fluid (osmolality) is maintained as well. If this were not the case, an increase in extracellular osmolality (an increase in the concentrations of electrolytes outside of cells) would result in the movement of intracellular fluid across the cell membrane into the extracellular fluid. Because the kidneys would excrete much of the fluid from the expanded extracellular volume, dehydration would occur. Conversely, decreased serum osmolality (a decrease in the concentrations of electrolytes outside of cells) would lead to a buildup of fluid within the cells.

Another homeostatic mechanism involves the maintenance of plasma volume. If the total volume of fluid within the circulation increases (overhydration), the pressure against the walls of the blood vessels and the heart increases, stimulating sensitive areas in heart and vessel walls to release hormones. These hormones, called natriuretic hormones, increase the excretion of water and electrolytes by the kidney, thus reducing the plasma volume to normal.

Hormonal systems also provide for the homeostasis of nutrients and fuels that are needed for body metabolism. For example, the blood glucose concentration is closely regulated by several hormones to ensure that glucose is available when needed and stored when in abundance. After food is ingested, increased blood glucose concentrations stimulate the secretion of insulin. Insulin then stimulates the uptake of glucose by muscle tissue and adipose (fatty) tissue and inhibits the production of glucose by the liver. In contrast, during fasting, blood glucose concentrations and insulin secretion decrease, thereby increasing glucose production by the liver and decreasing glucose uptake by muscle tissue and adipose tissue and preventing greater reductions in blood glucose concentrations.

GROWTH AND DIFFERENTIATION

Despite the many mechanisms designed to maintain a constant internal environment, the organism itself is subject to change: it is born, it matures, and it ages. These changes are accompanied by many changes in the composition of body fluids and tissues. For example, the serum phosphate concentration in healthy children ranges from about 4 to 7 mg per 100 ml (1.1 to 2.1 millimole per litre [mmol/l]), whereas the concentration in normal adults ranges from about 3 to 4.5 mg per 100 ml (1 to 1.3 mmol/l). These and other more striking changes are part of a second major function of the endocrine system—namely, the control of growth and development. The mammalian fetus develops in the uterus of the mother in a system known as the fetoplacental unit. In this system the fetus is under the powerful influence of hormones from its own endocrine glands and hormones produced by the mother and the placenta. Maternal endocrine glands assure that a proper mixture of nutrients is transferred by way of the placenta to the growing fetus. Hormones also are present in the mother's milk and are transferred to the suckling young.

Sexual differentiation of the fetus into a male or a female is also controlled by delicately timed hormonal changes. Following birth and a period of steady growth in infancy and childhood, the changes associated with puberty and adolescence take place. This dramatic transformation of an adolescent into a physically mature adult is also initiated and controlled by the endocrine system. In addition, the process of aging and senescence in adults is associated with endocrine-related changes.

ADAPTIVE RESPONSES TO STRESS

Throughout life the endocrine system and the hormones it secretes enhance the ability of the body to respond to stressful internal and external stimuli. The endocrine system allows not only the individual organism but also the species to survive. Acutely threatened animals and humans respond to stress with multiple physical changes, including endocrine changes, that prepare them to react or retreat. This process is known as the "fight-or-flight" response. Endocrine changes associated with this response include increased secretion of cortisol by the adrenal cortex, increased secretion of glucagon by the islet cells of the pancreas, and increased secretion of epinephrine and norepinephrine by the adrenal medulla.

Adaptive responses to more prolonged stresses also occur. For example, in states of starvation or malnutrition, there is reduced production of thyroid hormone, leading to a lower metabolic rate. A low metabolic rate reduces the rate of the consumption of the body's fuel and thus reduces the rate of consumption of the remaining energy stores. This change has obvious survival value since death from starvation is deferred. Malnutrition also causes a decrease in the production of gonadotropins and sex steroids, reducing the need for fuel to support reproductive processes.

PARENTING BEHAVIOUR

The endocrine system, particularly the hypothalamus, the anterior pituitary, and the gonads, is intimately involved in reproductive behaviour by providing physical, visual, and olfactory (pheromonal) signals that arouse the sexual interest of males and the sexual receptivity of females. Furthermore, there are powerful endocrine influences on parental behaviour in all species, including humans. For example, the hormone prolactin initiates and sustains lactation in women with newborns.

INTEGRATIVE FUNCTIONS

The endocrine systems of humans and other animals serve an essential integrative function. Inevitably, humans are beset by a variety of insults, such as trauma, infection, tumour formation, genetic defects, and emotional damage. The endocrine glands play a key role in mediating and ameliorating the effects of these insults on the body. Subtle changes in the body's fluids, although less obvious, also have important effects on storage and expenditure of

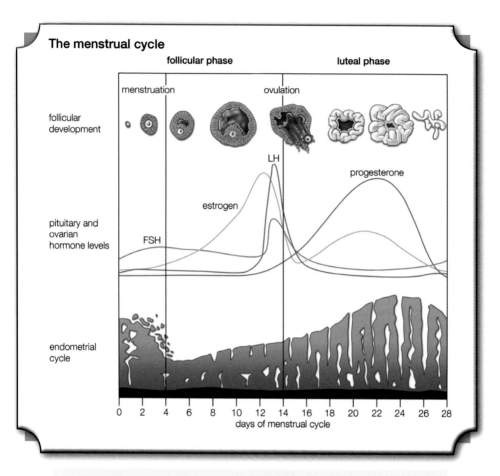

The menstrual cycle. Encyclopædia Britannica, Inc.

energy and steady and timely growth and development. These subtle changes largely result from the constant monitoring and measured response of the endocrine system.

The menstrual cycle in women and the reproductive process in men and women are under endocrine control. The endocrine system works in concert with the nervous system and the immune system. When functioning properly, these three systems direct the orderly progression of human life and protect and defend against threats to health and survival.

SYNTHESIS AND TRANSPORT OF HORMONES

Depending on the endocrine gland, hormone synthesis can be effected in any of several ways. For example, in some instances, the synthetic process entails cellular uptake of a specific nutrient or other substance that is a central component of the hormone. The final hormone is produced following a series of enzymatic reactions. In other cases, the binding of a protein to a receptor on the cell surface or in the cell interior triggers the production of a precursor hormone inside the cell via genetic mechanisms. Enzymes then cleave the precursor into the final hormone product.

Once synthesized, hormones often remain stored within cells and are released (secreted) only upon stimulation by a specific signal. Release, or secretion, from a cell marks the beginning of the transport phase. The distances and mechanisms by which hormones are transported are influenced primarily by the tissues to which the hormones are targeted.

HORMONE SYNTHESIS

Endocrine cells are rather homogeneous in appearance and are usually cuboidal in shape. When viewed under an electron microscope (a microscope of extraordinary magnifying power), the fine, detailed structure of endocrine cells can be seen. Many of the various intracellular structures, called organelles, are involved in the sequence of events that occurs during the synthesis and secretion of hormones. In the case of protein hormone synthesis, the target cell is stimulated when a hormone or other substance binds to a receptor on the surface of the cell. For example, growth hormone-releasing hormone binds to receptors on the surface of anterior pituitary cells to stimulate the synthesis and secretion of growth hormone. In some cases, protein hormone synthesis can be stimulated by the entrance of a metabolite (a substance produced during metabolism) into the cytoplasm or nucleus of a target cell. This type of stimulation occurs when glucose enters insulin-producing beta cells in the islets of Langerhans of the pancreas. There are also hormones and metabolites that lead to the inhibition of specific cellular activities. For example, dopamine is released from neurons and binds to receptors on lactotrophs in the anterior pituitary to inhibit the secretion of prolactin. (Lactotrophs are cells that synthesize and secrete prolactin.)

The stimulation of a receptor at the cell surface is followed by a series of complex events within the cell membrane. Events that occur within the cell membrane then stimulate activities within the cell that lead to the activation of specific genes in the nucleus. Genes contain unique sequences of DNA that code for specific protein hormones or for enzymes that direct the synthesis of other hormones. The transcription of genes results in the formation of messenger ribonucleic acid (mRNA) molecules.

In the case of hormone stimulation, the mRNA molecules contain the translated code required for synthesis of the target protein hormone (or enzyme). When mRNA leaves the nucleus and associates with an organelle called the endoplasmic reticulum in the cytoplasm, it directs the synthesis of a relatively inert precursor to the hormone, called a prohormone, from amino acids available within the cytoplasm. The prohormone is then transported to an organelle called the Golgi apparatus, where it is packaged into vesicles known as secretory granules. As the granules migrate to the cell surface the prohormone is cleaved by a special enzyme called a proteolytic enzyme that separates the inactive region from the active region of the hormone. Through a process known as exocytosis, the active hormone is discharged through the cell wall into the extracellular fluid. It should be noted that the same signal that increases the synthesis of a protein hormone usually also increases the immediate release of hormone from already synthesized secretory granules into the extracellular fluid.

The precursor of all steroid hormones, cholesterol, is produced in nonendocrine tissues (e.g., the liver) or is obtained from the diet. The cholesterol is then taken up by the adrenal gland and the gonads and is stored in vesicles within the cytoplasm. Through the actions of several enzymes, cholesterol is converted into steroid hormones.

The first step in steroid hormone synthesis is the conversion of cholesterol into pregnenolone, which occurs in mitochondria (organelles that produce most of the energy used for cellular processes). This conversion is mediated by a cleavage enzyme, the synthesis of which is stimulated in the adrenal glands by adrenocorticotropin (ACTH, or corticotropin) or angiotensin and in the ovaries and testes by follicle-stimulating hormone (FSH) and luteinizing hormone (LH). Adrenocorticotropin, angiotensin, follicle-stimulating hormone, and luteinizing hormone also stimulate the production of enzymes required for later steps in steroid hormone synthesis. Once pregnenolone is formed, it is transported out of the mitochondria and into the endoplasmic reticulum, where it undergoes further enzymatic conversion to progesterone. Progesterone is then converted into specific steroid hormones. For example, in the ovaries and testes, progesterone is converted into androgens and estrogens, and in the adrenal cortex, progesterone is converted into

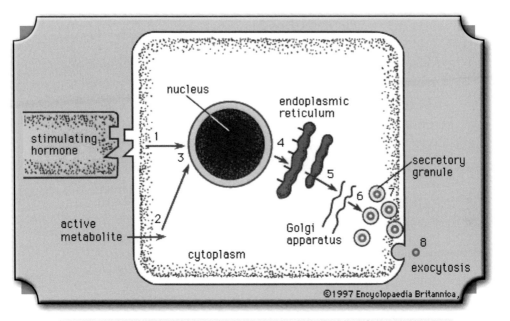

Intracellular structure of a typical endocrine cell. The process of protein hormone synthesis begins when a hormone or an active metabolite stimulates a receptor in the cell membrane. This leads to the activation of specific molecules of DNA in the nucleus and the formation of a prohormone. The prohormone is transported through the endoplasmic reticulum, is packaged into secretory vesicles in the Golgi apparatus, and is ultimately secreted from the cell in its active, hormone form.

androgens, mineralocorticoids, which regulate salt and water metabolism, and glucocorticoids, which stimulate the breakdown of fat and muscle to metabolites that can be converted to glucose in the liver.

The process of thyroid hormone synthesis is mediated by several enzymes. The synthesis of these enzymes is stimulated by the anterior pituitary hormone thyrotropin (thyroid-stimulating hormone, or TSH). Thyroid hormone synthesis is unique in that it requires iodine, which is available only from the diet, and it occurs within an already synthesized protein known as thyroglobulin. Thyroglobulin also serves as a storage protein and must be broken down to release thyroid hormone.

MODES OF HORMONE TRANSPORT

Most hormones are secreted into the general circulation to exert their effects on appropriate distant target tissues. There are important exceptions, however, such as self-contained portal circulations in which blood is directed to a specific area. A portal circulation begins in a capillary bed. As the capillaries extend away from the capillary bed, they merge to form a set of veins, which then divide to form a second capillary bed. Thus, blood collected from the first capillary bed is directed solely into the tissues nourished by the second capillary bed.

Two portal circulations in which hormones are transported are present in the human body. One system, the hypothalamic-hypophyseal portal circulation, collects blood from capillaries originating in the hypothalamus and, through a plexus of veins surrounding the pituitary stalk, directs the blood into the anterior pituitary gland. This allows the neurohormones secreted by the neuroendocrine cells of the hypothalamus to be transported directly to the cells of the anterior pituitary. These hormones are largely, but not entirely, excluded from the general circulation. In the second system, the hepatic portal circulation, capillaries originating in the gastrointestinal tract and the spleen merge to form the portal vein, which enters the liver and divides to form portal capillaries. This allows hormones from the islets of Langerhans of the pancreas, such as insulin and glucagon, as well as certain nutrients absorbed from the intestine, to be transported into the liver before being distributed through the general circulation.

In serum, many hormones exist both as free, unbound hormone and as hormone bound to a serum carrier or transport protein. These proteins, which are produced by the liver, bind to specific hormones in the serum. Transport proteins include sex hormone-binding globulin, which binds estrogens and androgens; corticosteroid-binding globulin, which binds cortisol; and growth hormone-binding protein, which binds growth hormone. There are two specific thyroid hormone binding proteins, thyroxine-binding globulin and transthyretin (thyroxine-binding prealbumin), and at least six binding proteins for insulin-like growth factor-i (IGF-i).

In serum, protein-bound hormones are in equilibrium with a much smaller concentration of free, unbound hormones. As free hormone leaves the circulation to exert its action on a tissue, bound hormone is immediately freed from its binding protein. Thus, the transport proteins serve as a reservoir within the circulation to maintain a normal concentration of the biologically important free hormone. In addition, transport proteins protect against sudden surges in hormone secretion and facilitate even distribution of a hormone to all of the cells of large organs such as the liver. The production of many transport proteins is hormone-dependent, being increased by estrogens and decreased by androgens. However, the biological importance of this sensitivity to sex steroids is not well understood.

The affinity (attraction) of hormones for binding proteins is not constant. The thyroid hormone thyroxine, for example, binds much more tightly to thyroxine-binding globulin than does triiodothyronine. Therefore, triiodothyronine is readily released as a free molecule and has easier access to tissues than thyroxine. Similarly, among the sex steroids, testosterone binds more tightly to sex hormone-binding globulin than do other androgens or estrogens.

Biorhythms

Almost all of the body's physiological processes have a rhythm, or pattern, that varies over the course of a day. The most obvious of these circadian rhythms are sleep and wakefulness. The internal body clock also controls alertness, hunger, digestion, urine production, body temperature, and the secretion of hormones.

Some hormones, such as insulin, are secreted in short pulses every few minutes. Presumably, the time between pulses is a reflection of the lag time necessary for the insulin-secreting cell to sense a change in the blood glucose concentration. Other hormones, particularly those of the pituitary, are secreted in pulses that may occur at one- or two-hour intervals. Pulsatile secretion is a necessary requirement for the action of pituitary gonadotropins. For example, pituitary gonadotropin secretion increases substantially and is maintained at increased levels when gonadotropin-producing cells (gonadotrophs) are stimulated at 90- to 120-minute intervals by the injection of hypothalamic gonadotropin-releasing hormone. If, however, the gonadotrophs are subjected to a continuous injection of gonadotropin-releasing hormone, gonadotropin secretion is inhibited.

In addition to pulses of secretion, many hormones are secreted at different rates at different times of the day and night or over even longer cycles. Day-night periodic changes are called circadian rhythms. An example of a longer cycle is the woman's menstrual cycle, which occurs monthly and hence is a monthly biorhythm.

Circadian Rhythm

Circadian rhythm is the cyclical 24-hour period of human biological activity. Within the circadian cycle, a person usually sleeps for approximately 6 to 8 hours and is awake for 16 to 18 hours. During the wakeful hours, mental and physical functions are most active and tissue cell growth increases. During sleep, voluntary muscle activities nearly disappear and there is a decrease in metabolic rate, respiration, heart rate, body temperature, and blood pressure. The activity of the digestive system increases during the resting period, but that of the urinary system decreases. Hormones secreted by the body, such as the stimulant epinephrine (adrenaline), are released in maximal amounts about two hours before awakening so that the body is prepared for activity.

The circadian cycle is controlled by a region of the brain known as the hypothalamus, which is the master centre for integrating rhythmic information and establishing sleep patterns. A part of the hypothalamus called the suprachiasmatic nucleus (SCN) receives signals about light and dark from the retina of the eye. Upon activation by light, special photoreceptor cells in the retina transmit signals to the SCN via neurons of the retinohypothalamic tract. The signals are further transmitted to the pineal gland, a small cone-shaped structure that is attached to the posterior end (behind the hypothalamus) of the third cerebral ventricle and that is responsible for the production of a hormone called melatonin. Cyclical fluctuations of melatonin are vital for maintaining a normal circadian rhythm. When the retina detects light, melatonin production is inhibited and wakefulness ensues. Light wavelength (colour) and intensity are important factors affecting the extent to which melatonin production is inhibited. In contrast, in response to darkness, melatonin production is increased, and the body begins to prepare for sleep. Sleep-inducing reactions, such as decreases in body temperature and blood pressure, are generated when melatonin binds to receptors in the SCN.

Another example of a circadian rhythm is that of cortisol, the major steroid hormone produced by the adrenal cortex. Serum cortisol concentrations rapidly increase in the early morning hours, gradually decrease during the day, with small elevations after meals, and remain decreased for much of the night. This particular rhythm is dependent on night-day cycles and persists for some days after airplane travel to different time zones.

Other hormones follow different circadian rhythms. For example, serum concentrations of growth hormone, thyrotropin, and the gonadotropins are highest shortly after the onset of sleep. In the case of gonadotropins, this sleep-related increase is the first biochemical sign of the onset of puberty.

The natural time signal for the circadian pattern is the change from darkness to light. Where daylight patterns are not consistent, as in outer space, regimented cycles are established to simulate the 24-hour day. If one tries to break the circadian rhythm by ignoring sleep for a number of days, psychological disorders begin to arise. The human body can learn to function in cycles ranging between 18 and 28 hours, but any variance greater or less than this usually causes the body to revert to a 24-hour cycle. Even in totally lighted areas such as the subpolar twilight zone, the body has regular cycles of sleep and wakefulness once the initial adjustment has been made.

The circadian cycle can alter the effectiveness of some drugs. For example, the timing of administration of hormonal drugs so as to be in accord with their natural circadian production pattern seems to place less stress on the body and produce more effective medical results.

Jet Lag

Jet lag is a physiological desynchronization caused by transmeridian (east-west) travel between different time zones. The severity and extent of jet lag vary according to the number of time zones crossed as well as the direction of travel—most people find it difficult to travel eastward (i.e., to adapt a shorter day as opposed to a longer one). The resulting symptoms include extreme fatigue, sleep disturbances, loss of concentration, disorientation, malaise, sluggishness, gastrointestinal upset, and loss of appetite. In general, adjustment to a new time zone takes one day for each hour of time difference.

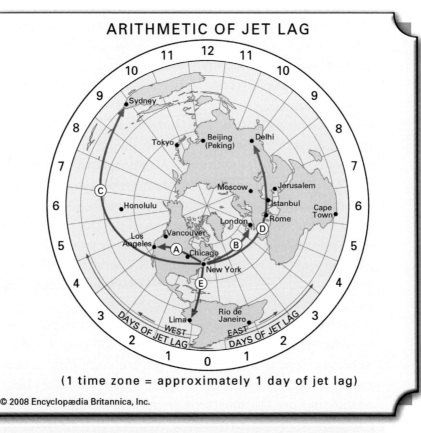

ARITHMETIC OF JET LAG

(1 time zone = approximately 1 day of jet lag)

© 2008 Encyclopædia Britannica, Inc.

Map showing travel from New York City to cities around the world. Each number corresponds to one time zone and roughly one day of jet lag. Flight A goes from New York to Los Angeles and crosses three time zones; flight B, to London, crosses five time zones; flight C, to Sydney, spans nine time zones; and flight D, to Delhi, crosses 10 time zones. Flight E, to Lima, crosses only one time zone.

Cortisol is particularly sensitive to interruptions in sleep-wake cycles and is found in unusually high levels in people who experience jet lag on a regular basis (e.g., flight attendants and pilots). Brain scans and memory performance tests of such crew members, who often work multiple transmeridian flights with brief in-between flight "recovery" times, show that they have reduced temporal lobes and poor short-term memory. Increasing cortisol levels corresponded with decreasing temporal lobe size in these individuals, suggesting a direct link between physiological desynchronization and decreased functionality of short-term memory. Fortunately, once synchronization is reestablished, short-term memory returns to its normal state.

Because long-distance transmeridian jet travelers normally experience a significant shift in the light-dark cycles, melatonin secretion is also immediately "out of sync" upon arrival in a new time zone. Studies have shown that judicious and carefully timed light exposure has a dramatic effect in alleviating jet lag. In addition, administration of melatonin offers a direct and practicable way of actually accelerating the resynchronization of the body clock to a new time zone. Although melatonin has been widely studied and appears to be effective and safe, it has not been evaluated or licensed by the U.S. Food and Drug Administration (FDA).

Frequent travelers often develop their own strategies for managing jet lag, and following several simple guidelines can lessen symptoms of jet lag significantly. For example, during westbound flights, which have the effect of lengthening the day, naps should be avoided. In contrast, while flying eastbound, which has the effect of shortening the day, sleeping during flight is encouraged. In addition, daytime flights cause the least loss of sleep and the least fatigue, allowing the traveler to arrive in the best possible condition. It is most efficient to overcome jet lag by adjusting to the new time zone as soon as possible. This can be done simply by eating meals and going to bed at appropriate times and by spending plenty of time outdoors during the day. While flying, the consumption of alcohol and caffeine, which can interfere with sleep, should be avoided. Finally, the traveler should accept that there is bound to be some loss of performance when first arriving in a new time zone and should plan accordingly. For example, one should avoid important business meetings for the first 24 hours after arrival.

FEEDBACK REGULATION MECHANISMS OF ENDOCRINE SIGNALING

A constant supply of most hormones is essential for health, and sustained increases or decreases in hormone production often lead to disease. Many hormones are produced at a relatively constant rate, and in healthy individuals the day-to-day serum concentrations of these hormones lie within a rather narrow normal range. However, hormone concentrations in the circulation may change in response to stimulatory or inhibitory influences that act on the hormone-producing cells or to increases or decreases in the degradation or excretion of the hormones.

Hormone production and serum hormone concentrations are maintained by feedback mechanisms. Target glands, such as the thyroid gland, adrenal glands, and gonads, are under distant feedback regulation by the hypothalamic-pituitary-target gland axis. Other hormonal systems, however, are under direct feedback regulation mechanisms. For example, serum calcium concentrations are detected directly by calcium receptors in the parathyroid glands, and blood glucose concentrations are detected directly by the beta cells of the islets of Langerhans. The metabolism of hormones after their secretion also serves as a mechanism of hormone regulation and may result in either an increase or a decrease in hormone activity. For example, thyroxine (T_4) may be converted to triiodothyronine (T_3), a change that substantially increases its hormonal potency, or it may be converted to reverse triiodothyronine (reverse T_3), a molecule with the same three iodine atoms that has minimal biological activity.

GROWTH AND DEVELOPMENT

The processes of growth and development are governed by many factors, including the inherent capacity of tissues for growth and differentiation, the hormonal influence of the endocrine system, and the stimulatory signals from the nervous system. In the amount of time from the 10th to the 20th week of pregnancy, the fetus grows 12.7 cm (5 inches) in length. This phenomenal growth rate slows dramatically as birth approaches. Birth weight is an important marker of nutrition during gestation and an important predictor of growth following birth. Low birth weight is common among infants of mothers whose family histories include low birth weight, and it may also be an indication of premature birth or of poor intrauterine nourishment. Rapid growth occurs during infancy and then slows until the onset of puberty, when it increases strikingly for several years. The pubertal growth spurt lasts 2 to 3 years, and it is accompanied by the appearance of secondary sexual characteristics. The pubertal growth spurt is associated with both an increase in nocturnal secretion of growth hormone and an increase in serum concentrations of sex steroids. The growth potential of a child can be estimated with moderate accuracy from measurements of the child's height and the heights of the parents and from measurements of the child's skeletal, or bone, age.

Accurate estimates of bone age in children can be made from X-rays of the hands and wrists. These X-rays reveal the extent of maturation of the epiphyses (growth centres) of bones, which allows the bone age of the child being examined to be compared with the bone age of healthy children of the same chronological age. In children with endocrine disorders, bone age may not correlate closely with chronological age. For example, bone age is delayed in children with growth hormone deficiency and accelerated in children with growth hormone-producing tumours. Excess production of androgens or estrogens in childhood is associated with an increase in growth rate and an acceleration of epiphyseal maturation so that bone age is advanced. The excess production of androgens and estrogens ultimately causes premature closure of the epiphyses and short stature. Deficiency of androgens and estrogens during crucial periods of growth in childhood leads to a delay in epiphyseal maturation (retarded bone age), and, consequently, in adulthood affected individuals have long arms and long legs and a normal trunk (eunuchoid habitus, or height that is equal to or less than arm span).

CHAPTER 2

MAJOR ENDOCRINE HORMONES AND EVALUATION OF ENDOCRINE FUNCTION

Hormones are the messengers of the endocrine system. They relay important information between glands, facilitating the body's response to change or stress. The ability of hormones to fulfill their roles as messengers depends on a range of processes, including synthesis and transport. The mechanisms by which these processes are carried out in turn depends primarily on which endocrine gland is responsible for the hormone's synthesis and on the tissue in which the hormone will exert its effects. The following sections of this chapter explore the synthesis, transport, and action of major hormones of the endocrine system, as well as their clinical evaluation for the diagnosis of disease.

MAJOR ENDOCRINE HORMONES OF GROWTH AND METABOLISM

There are a number of endocrine hormones, and each has a specific effect on its target tissue. These hormones are synthesized in and released from a wide variety of endocrine glands. Examples of major endocrine hormones include cortisol, growth hormone, melatonin, and thyrotropin (thyroid-stimulating hormone).

ADRENOCORTICOTROPIC HORMONE

Adrenocorticotropic hormone (ACTH; also called corticotropin, or adrenocorticotropin) is a polypeptide hormone (a long molecular chain of amino acids) formed in the pituitary gland that regulates the activity of the outer region (cortex) of the adrenal glands.

In mammals the action of adrenocorticotropin is limited to those areas of the adrenal cortex in which the glucocorticoid hormones—cortisol and corticosterone—are formed. The secretion of adrenocorticotropin by the pituitary is itself regulated by another polypeptide, corticotropin-releasing hormone (CRH), which is discharged from the hypothalamus in the brain in response to impulses transmitted by the nervous system.

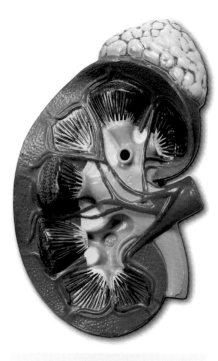

In humans the kidneys are located on either side of the backbone and are even with the lowest ribs. Kidneys maintain water balance and expel metabolic waste. Shutterstock.com

Adrenocorticotropin is a segment of a much larger glycoprotein prohormone molecule called proopiomelancortin (POMC). Proopiomelanocortin is synthesized by the corticotrophs of the anterior pituitary, which constitute about 10 percent of the gland. The molecule is split into several biologically active polypeptides when the secretory granules (material created inside a cell for secretion outside of it) are discharged from the corticotrophs. Among these polypeptides is adrenocorticotropin, whose major action is to stimulate the growth and secretion of the cells of the adrenal cortex. In addition, the hormone causes an increase in skin pigmentation. Other polypeptides derived from proopiomelanocortin include melanocyte-stimulating hormone (alpha- and beta-melanotropin), which increases skin pigmentation; beta-lipotropin, which stimulates the release of fatty acids from adipose tissue; a small fragment of adrenocorticotropin, which is thought to improve memory; and beta-endorphin, which suppresses pain.

Increased secretion of adrenocorticotropin because of a corticotroph tumour or corticotroph hyperplasia causes adrenocortical hyperfunction. Adrenocorticotropin deficiency can occur as part of a multiple pituitary hormone deficiency syndrome or as an isolated deficiency.

CALCITONIN

Calcitonin, also known as thyrocalcitonin, is a protein hormone secreted in humans by parafollicular cells (C cells) in the thyroid gland. Calcitonin lowers the concentration of calcium in the blood when it rises above the normal value. This effect is the opposite of that of parathyroid hormone. Calcitonin is a protein containing 32 amino acids that is synthesized by and secreted from parafollicular cells. Parafollicular cells lie between the thyroid follicular cells, and, during embryonic development, these cells migrate into the substance of the thyroid gland from a fetal structure called a branchial pouch.

Calcitonin acts to decrease serum calcium concentrations by inhibiting the activity of the osteoclasts (cells responsible for the dissolution and absorption of bone) in bone tissue and by increasing calcium excretion in the urine. However, both increased calcitonin secretion and increased calcitonin activity are very short-lived, lasting only a few days. As a result, patients with chronically high serum calcium concentrations (hypercalcemia) do not have high serum calcitonin concentrations.

CORTICOTROPIN-RELEASING HORMONE

Corticotropin-releasing hormone (CRH) is a peptide hormone that stimulates both the synthesis and the secretion of adrenocorticotropin in the corticotropin-producing cells of the anterior pituitary gland. Corticotropin-releasing hormone consists of a single chain of 41 amino acids. Many factors of neuronal and hormonal origin regulate the secretion of corticotropin-releasing hormone, and it is the final common element that directs the body's response to many forms of stress, including physical and emotional stresses and external and internal stresses.

In healthy individuals adrenocorticotropin is secreted in a circadian rhythm, which in turn causes pulsatile and diurnal (daily) secretion of cortisol. Variations in the secretion of adrenocorticotropin are caused by variations in the secretion of corticotropin-releasing hormone by the hypothalamus in the brain as well as by variations in serum cortisol concentrations. An increase in serum cortisol inhibits the secretion of both corticotropin-releasing hormone and adrenocorticotropin. Conversely, the secretion of these hormones is increased when serum levels of cortisol decrease, thereby restoring to normal the serum concentrations of cortisol.

Excessive secretion of corticotropin-releasing hormone leads to an increase in the size and number of corticotrophs in the pituitary gland. This may result in the formation of a corticotroph tumour that produces excessive amounts of adrenocorticotropin, resulting in overstimulation of the adrenal cortex and abnormally high serum concentrations of adrenal androgens as well as cortisol. Excessive secretion of cortisol causes Cushing syndrome, which is characterized by trunk and facial obesity, high blood pressure (hypertension), and generalized protein breakdown, causing skin and muscle atrophy and loss of bone. In contrast, a deficiency of corticotropin-releasing hormone can, by decreasing adrenocorticotropin secretion, cause adrenocortical deficiency.

CORTISOL

Cortisol (also known as hydrocortisone) is an organic compound belonging to the steroid family that is the principal hormone secreted by the adrenal glands. It is a potent anti-inflammatory agent and is used for the palliative treatment of diseases such as rheumatoid arthritis.

Cortisol is the major glucocorticoid in humans. It has two primary actions: stimulating gluconeogenesis—the breakdown of protein and fat to provide metabolites that can be converted to glucose in the

Many important physiological functions of vertebrates are controlled by steroid hormones. Encyclopædia Britannica, Inc.

liver—and activating antistress and anti-inflammatory pathways. It also has weak mineralocorticoid activity (activity that affects electrolyte and fluid balance in the body). Cortisol plays a major role in the body's response to stress. It helps to maintain blood glucose concentrations by increasing gluconeogenesis and by blocking the uptake of glucose into tissues other than the central nervous system. It also contributes to the maintenance of blood pressure by augmenting the constrictive effects of catecholamines (e.g., epinephrine, norepinephrine, and dopamine) that function as hormones or neurotransmitters or both on blood vessels.

Cortisol—along with more-potent and longer-acting synthetic derivatives such as prednisone, methylprednisolone, and dexamethasone—has powerful anti-inflammatory and antiallergy actions. At a cellular level, glucocorticoids inhibit the production and action of inflammatory cytokines, small, short-lived proteins that are released by one cell to regulate the function of another cell. In high doses, glucocorticoids can impair the function of the immune system, thereby reducing cell-mediated immune reactions and reducing the production and action of antibodies. Reducing immune system function with glucocorticoids is useful for preventing transplant rejection and for treating allergic or autoimmune diseases, such as rheumatoid arthritis and disseminated lupus erythematosus. However, these beneficial effects are offset by the serious side effects of high doses of glucocorticoids, especially when administered over a long period of time. The manifestations of chronic exposure of the body to excess levels of glucocorticoids can be seen in patients with Cushing syndrome. In addition, glucocorticoids are generally not used in patients with infectious diseases because immunosuppressive and anti-inflammatory actions may allow the infection to spread.

Cortisol exists in serum in two forms. The majority of cortisol is in the bound form, attached to cortisol-binding globulin (transcortin), while the remaining amount of cortisol is in the free, or unbound, form. As the free cortisol leaves the serum to enter cells, the pool of free cortisol in the serum is replenished by cortisol that is released from transcortin or new cortisol that is secreted from the adrenal cortex. In the cytoplasm of a target cell, cortisol binds to a specific receptor. The cortisol-receptor complex then enters the nucleus of the cell. In the nucleus the complex activates or inhibits the transcription of specific genes, thereby altering the production of messenger ribonucleic acid (mRNA) molecules that direct the synthesis of many proteins, including enzymes and structural proteins.

In contrast to cortisol, aldosterone and adrenal androgens do not bind as readily to serum proteins. While small amounts of cortisol and other steroid hormones are excreted in the urine, the majority of these hormones are inactivated in the liver or other tissues.

GONADOTROPIN

Gonadotropin is any of several hormones occurring in vertebrates that are secreted from the anterior pituitary gland and that act on the gonads (i.e., the ovaries or testes). Gonadotrophs, cells that constitute about 10 percent of the pituitary gland, secrete two primary gonadotropins: luteinizing hormone (LH) and follicle-stimulating hormone (FSH). The amount and rate of secretion of these hormones vary widely at different ages and at different times during the menstrual cycle in women. Secretion of LH and FSH is low in both males and females prior to puberty. Following puberty, more LH than FSH is secreted. During the menstrual cycle there is a dramatic increase in the serum concentrations of both hormones at the time of ovulation, and the secretion of both hormones increases 10- to 15-fold in postmenopausal women.

Another type of gonadotropin found in women is human chorionic gonadotropin (HCG), which is produced by the placenta during pregnancy. The detection of HCG forms the basis of pregnancy tests.

In men, FSH stimulates the development of spermatozoa, in large part by acting on special cells in the testes called Sertoli cells. LH stimulates the secretion of androgen (male) hormones by specialized cells in the testes called Leydig cells. In women, FSH stimulates the synthesis of estrogens and the maturation of cells lining the spherical egg-containing structures known as Graafian follicles. In menstruating women, there is a preovulatory surge in serum FSH and LH concentrations. The preovulatory surge of LH is essential for rupture of the Graafian follicle (ovulation), after which the egg enters the fallopian tube and travels to the uterus. The empty Graafian follicle becomes filled with progesterone-producing cells, transforming it into a corpus luteum. (A corpus luteum is a yellow, hormone-secreting body formed in an ovary at the site of a follicle.) LH stimulates the production of progesterone by the corpus luteum. Inhibin, a hormone secreted by the Graafian follicles of the ovaries and by the Sertoli cells of the testes, inhibits the secretion of FSH from the pituitary gonadotrophs.

Patients with diseases involving the anterior pituitary gland often have gonadotropin deficiency. Thus, the disappearance of menstrual periods may be the first sign of a pituitary tumour or other pituitary disease in women. In men the most common symptoms of gonadotropin deficiency are loss of libido and erectile dysfunction. Isolated deficiencies of both LH and FSH do occur but only rarely. In men isolated LH deficiency ("fertile eunuch") is characterized by symptoms and signs of androgen deficiency.

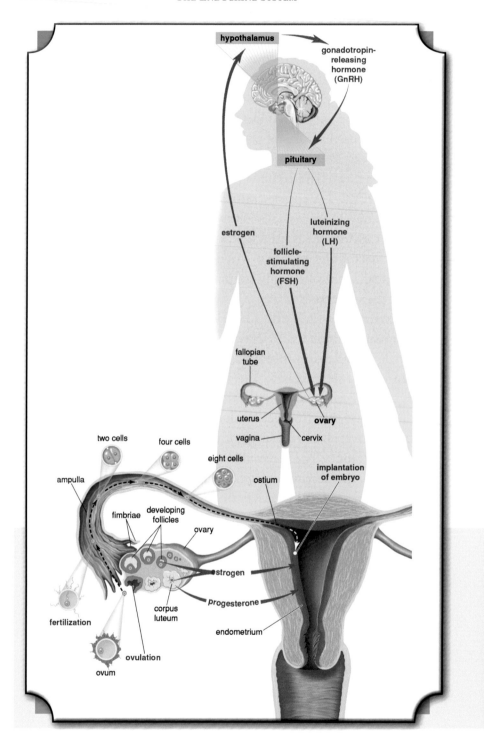

However, there is sufficient secretion of FSH to permit the maturation of spermatozoa. Some pituitary tumours produce an excess of LH or FSH, whereas other pituitary tumours produce the hormonally inactive alpha chain subunit of the glycoprotein hormones.

GONADOTROPIN-RELEASING HORMONE

Gonadotropin-releasing hormone (GnRH; or luteinizing hormone-releasing hormone) is a neurohormone consisting of 10 amino acids that is produced in the arcuate nuclei of the hypothalamus. GnRH stimulates the synthesis and secretion of the two gonadotropins—LH and FSH—by the anterior pituitary gland. The effects of GnRH on the secretion of LH and FSH are not exactly parallel, and the variations are probably due to other modulating factors such as the serum concentrations of steroid hormones (substances secreted by the adrenal cortex, testes, and ovaries).

Characteristic of all releasing hormones and most striking in the case of GnRH is the phenomenon of pulsatile secretion. Under normal circumstances, GnRH is released in pulses at intervals of about 90 to 120 minutes. In order to increase serum gonadotropin concentrations

The hypothalamus and pituitary gland control the secretion of gonadotropins (luteinizing hormone and follicle-stimulating hormone) that regulate the processes of ovulation and menstruation in women. Gonadotropin-releasing hormone is secreted from the hypothalamus in response to neuronal activity in the limbic region of the brain, which is predominantly influenced by emotional and sexual factors. Gonadotropin-releasing hormone stimulates the secretion of gonadotropins from the pituitary gland that then stimulate cells in the ovary to synthesize and secrete estrogen and progesterone. Increased serum concentrations of estrogen and progesterone provide negative feedback signaling in the hypothalamus to inhibit further secretion of gonadotropin-releasing hormone. Encyclopædia Britannica, Inc.

in patients with GnRH deficiency, the releasing hormone must be administered in pulses. In contrast, constant administration of GnRH suppresses gonadotropin secretion, which has therapeutic benefits in certain patients, such as children with precocious puberty and men with prostate cancer.

The neurons that secrete gonadotropin-releasing hormone have connections to an area of the brain known as the limbic system, which is heavily involved in the control of emotions and sexual activity. In rats that are deprived of their pituitary gland and ovaries but are given physiological amounts of estrogen, injection of GnRH results in changes in posture characteristic of the receptive female stance for sexual intercourse.

Hypogonadism, in which the functional activity of the gonads is decreased and sexual development is inhibited, can be caused by a congenital deficiency of GnRH. Patients with this type of hypogonadism typically respond to pulsatile treatment with the hormone. Many of these patients also have deficiencies of other hypothalamic-releasing hormones. A subset of patients with hypogonadism have isolated GnRH deficiency and loss of the sense of smell (anosmia). This disorder is called Kallmann syndrome and is usually caused by a mutation in a gene that directs the formation of the olfactory (sense of smell) system and the formation of parts of the hypothalamus. Abnormalities in the pulsatile secretion of GnRH result in subnormal fertility and abnormal or absent menstruation.

GROWTH HORMONE

Growth hormone (also called somatotropin) is a peptide hormone secreted by the anterior lobe of the pituitary gland. It stimulates the growth of essentially all tissues of the body, including bone. Growth hormone is synthesized and secreted by anterior pituitary cells called somatotrophs, which release between one and two milligrams of the hormone each day. Growth hormone is vital for normal physical growth in children. Its levels rise progressively during childhood and peak during the growth spurt that occurs in puberty.

In biochemical terms, growth hormone stimulates protein synthesis and increases fat breakdown to provide the energy necessary for tissue growth. It also antagonizes (opposes) the action of insulin. Growth hormone may act directly on tissues, but much of its effect is mediated by stimulation of the liver and other tissues to produce and release insulin-like growth factors, primarily insulin-like growth factor 1 (IGF-1).

Growth hormone secretion is stimulated by growth hormone-releasing hormone (GHRH) and is inhibited by somatostatin. In addition, growth hormone secretion is pulsatile, with surges in secretion occurring after the onset of deep sleep that are especially prominent at the time of puberty. In normal subjects, growth hormone secretion increases in response to decreased food intake and to physiological stresses and decreases in response to food ingestion. However, some individuals are affected by abnormalities in growth hormone secretion, which involve either deficiency or overabundance of the hormone.

GROWTH HORMONE-RELEASING HORMONE

Growth hormone-releasing hormone (GHRH) is a large peptide hormone that exists in several forms that differ from one another only in the number of amino acids, which can vary from 37 to 44. Unlike other neurohormones (substances produced by specialized cells typical of the nervous system), growth hormone-releasing hormone is not widely distributed throughout the brain and is found only in the hypothalamus. The secretion of growth hormone-releasing hormone increases in response to physical and emotional stress, and its secretion is blocked by a powerful hypothalamic neurohormone called somatostatin. The secretion of growth hormone-releasing hormone is also inhibited by insulin-like growth factors, which are generated when tissues are exposed to growth hormone itself.

Ghrelin, a 28-amino-acid peptide, is a hypothalamic substance that acts synergistically with growth hormone-releasing hormone to increase growth hormone secretion. Ghrelin may also stimulate the secretion of growth hormone-releasing hormone and inhibit the secretion of somatostatin. The physiologic role of ghrelin in the regulation of growth hormone secretion is not known.

INSULIN-LIKE GROWTH FACTOR

Insulin-like growth factor (IGF), formerly called somatomedin, is any of several peptide hormones that function primarily to stimulate growth but that also possess some ability to decrease blood glucose levels. IGFs were discovered when investigators began studying the effects of biological substances on cells and tissues outside the body. The name *insulin-like growth factor* reflects the fact that these substances have insulin-like actions in some tissues, though they are far less potent than insulin in decreasing blood glucose concentrations. Furthermore, their fundamental action is to stimulate growth, and, though IGFs share this ability with other growth factors—such as epidermal growth factor, platelet-derived growth factor, and nerve growth factor—IGFs differ from these substances in that they are the only ones with well-described endocrine actions in humans.

There are two IGFs: IGF-1 and IGF-2. These two factors, despite the similarity of their names, are distinguishable in terms of specific actions on tissues because they bind to and activate different receptors. The major action of IGFs is on cell growth. Indeed, most of the actions of pituitary growth hormone are mediated by IGFs, primarily IGF-1. Growth hormone stimulates many tissues, particularly the liver, to synthesize and secrete IGF-1, which in turn stimulates both hypertrophy (increase in cell size) and hyperplasia (increase in cell number) of most tissues, including bone. Serum IGF-1 concentrations progressively increase during childhood and peak at the time of puberty, and they progressively decrease thereafter (as does growth hormone secretion). Children and adults with deficiency of growth hormone have low serum IGF-1 concentrations compared with healthy individuals of the same age. In contrast, patients with high levels of growth hormone (e.g., persons affected by gigantism) have increased serum IGF-1 concentrations. The production of IGF-2 is less dependent on the secretion of growth hormone than is the production of IGF-1, and IGF-2 is much less important in stimulating linear growth.

Although serum IGF concentrations seem to be determined by production by the liver, these substances are produced by many tissues, and many of the same tissues also have receptors for them. In addition, there are multiple serum binding proteins for IGFs that may stimulate or inhibit the biological actions of the factors. It is likely that the growth-promoting actions of IGFs occur at or very near the site of their formation. In effect, they probably exert their major actions by way of paracrine (acting on neighbouring cells) and autocrine (self-stimulating) effects.

MELATONIN

Melatonin is a hormone secreted by the pineal gland, a tiny endocrine gland situated at the centre of the brain. Melatonin was discovered in 1958 by American physician Aaron B. Lerner and his colleagues at Yale University School of Medicine. Melatonin, a derivative of the amino acid tryptophan, is produced in humans, other mammals, birds, reptiles, and amphibians.

In humans, melatonin plays an important role in the regulation of circadian rhythm. Its production is influenced by the detection of light and dark by the retina of the eye. Melatonin generation by the pineal gland, which peaks during the nighttime hours, induces physiological changes that promote sleep, such as decreased body temperature and respiration rate. During the day, melatonin levels are low because large amounts of light are detected by the retina. Light inhibition of melatonin production is central to stimulating wakefulness in the morning and to maintaining alertness throughout the day.

Melatonin receptors are found in the suprachiasmatic nucleus (SCN) in the hypothalamus and in the pituitary gland of the brain, as well as in the ovaries, blood vessels, and intestinal tract. There is a high concentration of receptors in the SCN because this is where melatonin mediates the majority of its affects on circadian rhythm. The binding of melatonin to its receptors on the pituitary gland and the ovaries appears to play a role in regulating the release of reproductive hormones in females. For example, the timing, length, and frequency of menstrual cycles in women are influenced by melatonin. In addition, in certain mammals (other than humans), such as horses and sheep, melatonin acts as a breeding and mating cue, since it is produced in greater amounts in response to the longer nights of winter and less so during summer. Animals who time their mating or breeding to coincide with favourable seasons (such as spring) may depend on melatonin production as a kind of biological clock that regulates their reproductive cycles on the basis of the length of the solar day. In amphibians, melatonin stimulates a lightening of the skin.

Melatonin has antiaging properties. For example, it acts as an antioxidant, neutralizing harmful oxidative radicals, and it is capable of activating certain antioxidant enzymes. Melatonin production gradually declines with age, and its loss is associated with several age-related diseases. Melatonin also plays a role in modulating certain functions of the immune system.

OXYTOCIN

Oxytocin is a hormone used clinically to stimulate contractions of the uterus during labour, to control bleeding following delivery, and to stimulate the secretion of breast milk. Oxytocin was first synthesized (along with the related vasopressin, or antidiuretic hormone [ADH]) by American biochemist Vincent du Vigneaud in 1953, and he received the Nobel Prize for Chemistry in 1955 for this work. Synthetic oxytocin has since become widely used in obstetric practice. Natural oxytocin is secreted by the posterior pituitary gland, which holds and secretes oxytocin produced by the hypothalamus.

Smooth-muscle cells in the uterus contain proteins that bind specifically to oxytocin. The number of these oxytocin receptors increases during late pregnancy. Thus, injections of oxytocin are sometimes used to facilitate the labour process, since large amounts of the hormone cause smooth muscles in the wall of the uterus to contract, which in turn initiates labour. Oxytocin's effect on uterine smooth muscle is dependent on the presence of estrogen, and for that reason oxytocin has little effect on the uterus during the early stages of pregnancy. Near term, however, it is very effective and successfully produces uterine contractions in 80–90 percent of the women to whom it is administered.

Oxytocin activates the flow of milk from the breasts (milk letdown) by stimulating the contraction of muscle cells located near the milk-containing glands within seconds after an infant begins to suckle. Emotional influences can also increase oxytocin secretion so that the cry of a

Breastfeeding, also called nursing, releases the hormone oxytocin in the mother's endocrine system. Oxytocin is a chemical linked to feelings of calm and contentment. Jupiterimages/Brand X Pictures/Thinkstock

hungry baby may stimulate milk letdown. There are no known disorders associated with under- or overproduction of oxytocin.

PARATHORMONE

Parathormone (also known as parathyroid hormone) is a substance produced and secreted by the parathyroid glands that regulates serum calcium concentration. Under the microscope the parathormone-producing cells, called chief cells, isolated from the parathyroid glands, occur in sheets interspersed with areas of fatty tissue. Occasionally the cells are arranged in follicles similar to but smaller than those present in the thyroid gland. As with other protein hormones, parathormone is synthesized as a large, inactive prohormone. At the time of secretion the prohormone is split, and the active hormone (a protein containing 84 amino acids) is released from the inactive precursor.

The major determinant of parathormone secretion is the serum concentration of ionized calcium. Serum calcium concentration is monitored by calcium-sensing receptors located on the surface of the parathyroid cells. When serum calcium concentrations increase, more calcium binds to the receptors, causing a decrease in parathormone secretion. Conversely, when serum calcium concentrations decrease, decreased calcium receptor binding causes an increase in parathormone secretion. Magnesium controls parathormone secretion in a similar fashion.

Parathormone has multiple actions, all of which result in an increase in serum calcium concentration. For example, it activates large bone-dissolving cells called osteoclasts that mobilize calcium from bone tissue, and it stimulates the kidney tubules to reabsorb calcium from the urine. Parathormone also stimulates the kidney

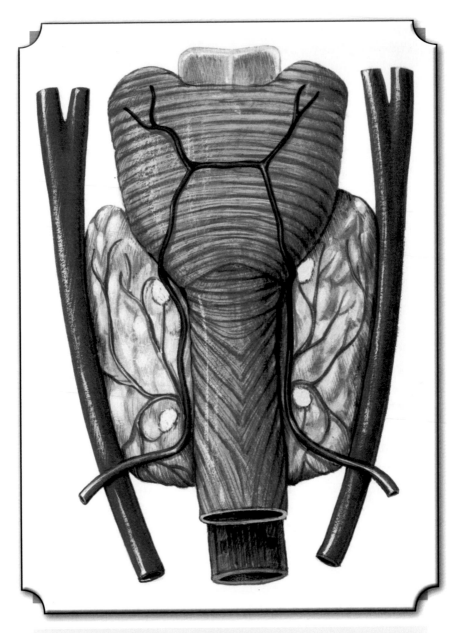

The parathyroid glands are located close to and behind the thyroid gland. Humans typically have four parathyroid glands, each one secreting para-thyroid hormone, which regulates blood calcium and phosphate levels. De Agostini/Getty Images

tubules to produce calcitriol (1,25-dihydroxyvitamin D), the most active form of vitamin D, from calcidiol (25-hydroxyvitamin D), a less active form of vitamin D. Calcitriol helps increase serum calcium concentrations because it stimulates the absorption of calcium from the gastrointestinal tract. Parathormone also inhibits the reabsorption of phosphate by the kidney tubules, thereby decreasing serum phosphate concentrations. This potentiates the ability of parathormone to increase serum calcium concentrations because fewer insoluble calcium-phosphate complexes are formed when serum phosphate concentrations are low.

Increased parathormone secretion is known as hyperparathyroidism and may be caused by a benign tumour in one of the parathyroid glands or by vitamin D deficiency or kidney disease. Decreased parathormone secretion, known as hypoparathyroidism, results from destruction or surgical removal of the parathyroid glands. A condition known as pseudohypoparathyroidism arises when kidney or bone tissues are resistant to parathormone.

SOMATOSTATIN

Somatostatin is a polypeptide that inhibits the activity of certain pancreatic and gastrointestinal hormones. Somatostatin exists in two forms: one composed of 14 amino acids and a second composed of 28 amino acids. The name *somatostatin*, essentially meaning stagnation of a body, was coined when investigators found that an extract of hypothalamic tissues inhibited the release of growth hormone from the pituitary gland. Somatostatin subsequently was found to be widely distributed throughout the central nervous system and to occur in other tissues.

In the pancreas, somatostatin is produced by the delta cells of the islets of Langerhans, where it serves to block the secretion of both insulin and glucagon from adjacent cells. Insulin, glucagon, and somatostatin act in concert to control the flow of nutrients into and out of the circulation. The relative concentrations of these hormones regulate the rates of absorption, utilization, and storage of glucose, amino acids, and fatty acids. The anatomic proximity of the beta, alpha, and delta cells in the islets of Langerhans is important. Somatostatin and glucagon appear to have a paracrine relationship, each influencing the secretion of the other, with both affecting the rate of insulin release. Somatostatin also inhibits the secretion of several gastrointestinal hormones—including gastrin, secretin, cholecystokinin (CCK), and vasoactive intestinal polypeptide (VIP)—resulting in the inhibition of many functions of the gastrointestinal tract, including the secretion of acid by the stomach, the secretion of digestive enzymes by the pancreas, and the absorption of nutrients by the intestine.

Few examples of somatostatin deficiency have been found. Alzheimer disease appears to cause a decrease in somatostatin levels in brain tissue, although it is not clear what role this plays in the course of the disease. In the late 1970s a rare somatostatin-producing tumour called a somatostatinoma was first identified. Since then somatostatinomas have been well characterized. The tumours tend to develop in the pancreas as well as in the first two portions of the small intestine—the duodenum and the jejunum. Diagnosis is based on plasma levels of a substance called somatostatin-like immunoreactivity (SLI), which may be 50 times greater than normal in individuals with a somatostatinoma. The excess levels of somatostatin may cause abdominal cramps and pain, persistent diarrhea, high blood glucose concentrations, weight loss, and episodic flushing of the skin.

THYROTROPIN

Thyrotropin (also known as thyroid-stimulating hormone, or TSH) is a substance produced by cells called thyrotrophs in the anterior pituitary gland. Thyrotropin binds to specific receptors on the surface of cells in the thyroid gland. This binding stimulates the breakdown of thyroglobulin (a large protein that is cleaved to form the thyroid hormones and that is stored within the follicles of the thyroid gland). The result is the secretion of the thyroid hormones thyroxine (T_4) and triiodothyronine (T_3) into the circulation.

Thyrotropin also stimulates the synthesis of additional thyroglobulin and thyroid hormone and the growth of thyroid cells. Thyrotropin is secreted by the pituitary gland upon the command of thyrotropin-releasing hormone. When thyrotropin causes the manufacture and secretion of excess thyroid hormone, the secreted hormone can travel to the pituitary gland and act on receptors that slow down the release of thyrotropin and hence thyrotropin-releasing hormone. This negative feedback contributes to the body's ability to maintain appropriate levels of thyroid hormones.

THYROTROPIN-RELEASING HORMONE

Thyrotropin-releasing hormone (TRH) is the simplest of the hypothalamic neurohormones, consisting of three amino acids in the sequence glutamic acid–histidine–proline. The structural simplicity of thyrotropin-releasing hormone is deceiving because this hormone actually has many functions. It stimulates the synthesis and secretion of thyrotropin by the anterior pituitary gland. Given in high doses by injection, it stimulates the secretion of prolactin from the pituitary gland, although it does not appear to regulate the secretion of prolactin. Thyrotropin-releasing hormone is also found throughout the brain and spinal cord, where it is thought to serve as a neuromodulator.

Thyrotropin-releasing hormone appeared very early in the evolution of vertebrates, and, while its concentration is highest in the hypothalamus, the total amount of thyrotropin-releasing hormone in the remainder of the brain far exceeds that in the hypothalamus. The nerve cells that produce thyrotropin-releasing hormone in the hypothalamus are subject to stimulatory and inhibitory influences from higher centres in the brain and from serum thyroid hormone concentrations, with low concentrations stimulating and high concentrations inhibiting the production of thyrotropin-releasing hormone. In this way, thyrotropin-releasing hormone forms the topmost component of the hypothalamic-pituitary-thyroid axis. Deficiency of thyrotropin-releasing hormone is a rare cause of hypothyroidism.

THYROXINE

Thyroxine (also called 3,5,3',5'-tetraiodothyronine, or T_4) is one of the two major hormones secreted by the thyroid gland (the other is triiodothyronine). Thyroxine's principal function is to stimulate the consumption of oxygen and thus the metabolism of all cells and tissues in the body. Thyroxine is formed by the molecular addition of iodine to the amino acid tyrosine while the latter is bound to the protein thyroglobulin. Excessive secretion of thyroxine in the body is known as hyperthyroidism, and the deficient secretion of it is called hypothyroidism. The chemical structure of thyroxine is

$$H_2N—\overset{\overset{\displaystyle H}{|}}{C}—COOH$$

thyroxine (Thy)
occurs only in the hormone protein
thyroglobulin: I= iodine

VASOPRESSIN

Vasopressin (or antidiuretic hormone) is a hormone that plays a key role in maintaining osmolality (the concentration of dissolved particles, such as salts and glucose, in the serum) and therefore in maintaining the volume of water in the extracellular fluid (the fluid space that surrounds cells). This is necessary to protect cells from sudden increases or decreases in water content, which are capable of interfering with proper cell function. Normal serum osmolality ranges from about 285 to 300 milliosmoles per kilogram (mOsm/kg) in healthy people. Vasopressin and oxytocin evolved from a single primordial neurohypophyseal hormone called vasotocin, which is present in lower vertebrates.

Special nerve cells called osmoreceptors in the hypothalamus are very sensitive to changes in serum osmolality. The osmoreceptors are closely associated with the same nerve cells that produce and secrete vasopressin. Serum osmolality that increases or decreases by as little as 1 percent can cause respective decreases or increases in vasopressin release. The immediate effect of an increase in serum osmolality—for example, if a person becomes dehydrated (e.g., loses water by excessive perspiration)— is a stimulation of the osmoreceptors. This stimulation leads to the separation of vasopressin from molecules of neurophysin, to which vasopressin is loosely attached within the secretory cells. Vasopressin is then released from the posterior pituitary gland, leading to the subsequent retention of water by the kidneys. Conversely, the immediate effect of a decrease in serum osmolality—for example, if a person becomes overhydrated (e.g., drinks too much water)—is the inhibition of the osmoreceptors. This inhibition leads to a decrease in vasopressin secretion and a subsequent increase in water excretion. The osmoreceptors are also closely linked to the thirst centre, which is stimulated by high serum osmolality and is inhibited by low serum osmolality in the same way as is vasopressin secretion.

In the kidneys, vasopressin acts on the cells of the collecting ducts. These cells contain receptors for vasopressin that are linked to vesicles that contain special water channels (aquaporins). When the cells are stimulated by vasopressin, the aquaporins fuse with the region of the cell membrane that is exposed to urine, allowing water to enter the cells. The water is then returned to the circulation. This causes the volume of urine to decrease and the urinary content of sodium, chloride, and other substances to increase. When this occurs, the urine is said to be concentrated.

Vasopressin is also released in response to a decrease in blood volume. Special pressure sensors called baroreceptors can detect arterial blood pressure. They are located in the carotid sinus, which is intimately associated with each carotid artery high in the neck, and in a group of specialized cells in the left atrium of the heart. When blood volume increases, the tissues of the carotid sinus and left atrium are stretched, and the nerves in the baroreceptors are stimulated. These nerves carry impulses to the vasopressin-producing nerve cells that inhibit the secretion of vasopressin, resulting in increased water excretion. Conversely, if blood volume decreases, the stretch of the carotid sinus and left atrium decreases, vasopressin release increases, and water excretion decreases, thereby helping to restore blood volume to normal. Other stimuli of vasopressin release include pain, stress, and several drugs, including opiate drugs.

SELECT TESTS FOR THE EVALUATION OF ENDOCRINE FUNCTION

The evaluation of endocrine function plays a fundamental role in the diagnosis of disease. In many instances, the simplest approach to determining whether a specific endocrine gland is functioning normally is to measure levels of the hormones associated with the gland, including those hormones to which the gland responds and those that it synthesizes and secretes. While not all hormones lend themselves to direct measurement, a number of tests have been developed for the detection of specific hormones.

To formulate an accurate diagnosis, physicians often evaluate the levels of all hormones associated with a gland. The findings derived from these tests, which may indicate hormone deficiency or excess, can then be used to inform approaches to treatment. Tests for endocrine function often are also used to evaluate whether a given treatment is effective.

Epinephrine Tolerance Test

Epinephrine tolerance tests assess the metabolism of liver glycogen by measuring the blood-sugar response to a standard dose of epinephrine (adrenalin). Epinephrine normally accelerates the conversion of liver glycogen (the conjugated, storage form of glucose) to blood glucose, and a blood-glucose rise of 40–60 mg per 100 ml of blood may be observed within one hour after a subcutaneous injection of epinephrine (usually 0.01 mg per kg [2.2 lb] of body weight), in subjects that have received a high-carbohydrate diet for three days before the test. Individuals with liver disease or with an inherited deficiency of the enzymes that degrade glycogen to glucose show a subnormal response. A modification of the test involves the substitution of a test dose of glucagon for epinephrine (glucagon tolerance test).

Glucose Tolerance Test

Glucose tolerance tests assess the ability of the body to metabolize glucose, the principal type of sugar found in the blood. In persons with normal or slightly elevated blood-sugar levels, the body tolerance to sugar is measured in a stressful situation induced by administering a large amount of glucose. The most common procedure is to take an initial blood sample from a fasting individual, have the individual empty his or her bladder, and then administer orally 50–100 grams of glucose (usually

1 gram of glucose per kilogram of ideal body weight) dissolved in water. Samples of blood and urine for glucose determination are obtained 30 minutes, 1 hour, 2 hours, and 3 hours later. Normally the concentration of glucose in the blood will rise to about 140 mg/100 ml within 45–60 minutes and will return in 1½–2½ hours to the normal range of 80–120 mg/100 ml. The most valuable diagnostic point is 2 hours, when the value should be less than 120 mg/100 ml.

A fasting glucose tolerance test can convey important information about decreased tolerance to sugar in persons suffering from an impairment of sugar metabolism, such as diabetes mellitus. In these individuals a decreased tolerance to sugar is manifested by a blood-sugar-level curve that rises higher than, and returns more slowly to, normal. This type of curve may also be seen in nondiabetic persons during acute illness, after trauma, or when on a low-carbohydrate diet. It may also be observed in elderly persons with hardening of the arteries or heart disease and in middle-aged persons who are markedly overweight.

An oral glucose tolerance test is used to confirm or exclude the diagnosis of diabetes mellitus when a fasting blood glucose test result is not definitive (i.e., greater than the upper range of the normal value but less than the diagnostic level for diabetes). Even if a blood glucose test is obtained after fasting 10–12 hours and the level is above 140 mg/100 ml, it is important to confirm the result with a second determination to rule out other factors that may have given a one-time abnormal test result.

The oral glucose tolerance test measures the response of the body to a challenge load (an amount calculated to evoke a response) of glucose. It most often is used during pregnancy to detect early glucose intolerance that could pose a significant risk to the infant if the condition progressed to gestational diabetes mellitus. After a fasting blood glucose test result has been obtained, 75 grams of glucose (100 g if the patient is pregnant) is administered and blood samples are taken every 30 minutes for 2 hours. In patients with diabetes, the blood glucose value will rise to a higher level and remain higher longer than in individuals who do not have diabetes.

A simpler but less-reliable screening test is the 2-hour postprandial blood glucose test. This test is performed 2 hours after intake of a standard glucose solution or a meal containing 100 grams of carbohydrates. A plasma glucose level above 140 mg/100 ml indicates the need for a glucose tolerance test.

THYROID FUNCTION TEST

Thyroid function tests assess the production of the two active thyroid hormones, thyroxine (T_4) and triiodothyronine (T_3), by the thyroid gland and the production of thyrotropin (TSH) by the pituitary gland. The best and most widely used tests are measurements of serum thyrotropin and thyroxine. The secretion of thyrotropin changes substantially in response to very small changes in thyroxine and triiodothyronine production. For example, small decreases in thyroid hormone production result in relatively large increases in serum concentrations of thyrotropin, and, conversely, small increases in thyroxine and triiodothyronine production result in relatively large decreases in serum concentrations of thyrotropin. Therefore, patients with hypothyroidism (thyroid deficiency) almost invariably have not only low serum thyroid hormone but also high serum thyrotropin concentrations, and those with hyperthyroidism have high serum thyroid hormone and low serum thyrotropin concentrations. An exception is patients with pituitary disease and thyrotropin deficiency, who have low serum thyroid hormone but normal or low serum thyrotropin concentrations. Between the two thyroid hormones, measurements of serum thyroxine are preferred because serum triiodothyronine concentrations are abnormal in many patients with nonthyroid illnesses.

Thyroxine and triiodothyronine exist in serum in two forms, bound and free (or unbound). Over 99 percent of each hormone is bound to one of three proteins—thyroxine-binding globulin, transthyretin (also known as thyroxine-binding prealbumin), and albumin. Serum thyroxine (and triiodothyronine) can be measured as the total hormone, which includes the bound and free fractions, or as free hormone alone. Changes in serum concentrations of these binding proteins occur, with the most common change being an increase in serum thyroxine-binding globulin in pregnant women and women taking estrogen. On the other hand, androgenic hormones and many illnesses decrease production of the binding proteins. These changes alter serum total thyroxine concentrations but not serum free thyroxine concentrations (and, similarly, total and free triiodothyronine concentrations). Thyroid hormone entry into tissues, and therefore hyperthyroidism or hypothyroidism, is correlated with serum free thyroxine and free triiodothyronine concentrations, not serum total thyroxine and total triiodothyronine concentrations. Therefore, measurements of serum free thyroxine are a better test for thyroid dysfunction than are measurements of serum total thyroxine.

The function of the thyroid is sometimes assessed by the radioactive iodine uptake test. In this test the patient is given an oral dose of radioactive iodine, and the fraction of the radioactive iodine that accumulates in the thyroid is measured 6 or 24 hours later. This test is used mostly to distinguish between different causes of hyperthyroidism. Radioactive iodine uptake is high in patients with hyperthyroidism caused by Graves disease or thyroid nodular disease, and it is low in patients with hyperthyroidism caused by thyroid inflammation.

While not a test of thyroid function, another common procedure is to measure several thyroid antibodies found in serum, namely antithyroid peroxidase antibodies, antithyroglobulin antibodies, and antibodies that act like thyrotropin (called TSH-receptor antibodies). Most patients with Hashimoto disease have high serum concentrations of antithyroid peroxidase and antithyroglobulin antibodies. Many patients with Graves disease have high serum concentrations of these two antibodies, as well as high serum concentrations of the TSH-receptor antibodies that cause the hyperthyroidism that characterizes the disease.

CHAPTER 3

Major Glands of the Endocrine System

The secretory organs that make up the human endocrine system, such as the anterior pituitary gland, the adrenal glands, and the pancreas, synthesize and secrete specific hormones. In addition, many endocrine glands, such as the thyroid gland, ovaries, and testes, are discrete, readily recognizable organs with defined borders and endocrine functions. Other endocrine glands, however, are embedded within structures. For example, the islets of Langerhans are embedded within the pancreas and may be seen clearly only under the microscope. The major glands and other anatomical considerations of the endocrine system are discussed in detail in this chapter.

ANATOMICAL CONSIDERATIONS

As already mentioned, the major organs of the endocrine system include the anterior pituitary, the adrenal glands, the pancreas, the thyroid gland, the ovaries, and the testes. Other body tissues may also function as endocrine organs. Examples include the lungs, the heart, the skeletal muscles, the kidneys, the lining of the gastrointestinal tract, and the bundles of nerve cells called nuclei. While all nerve cells are capable of secreting neurotransmitters into the synapses (small gaps) between adjacent nerves, nerve cells that regulate certain endocrine functions—for example, the nerve cells of the posterior pituitary gland (neurohypophysis)—secrete neurohormones directly into the bloodstream.

Sometimes, endocrine cells of different embryological origins that secrete different hormones reside side by side within a gland. The most obvious example of this is the existence of the parafollicular cells that reside among the thyroid follicular cells within the thyroid gland. Endocrine glands with mixed cell populations have not evolved by chance. The hormonal secretions of one type of cell may regulate the activity of adjacent cells that have different characteristics. This direct action on contiguous cells, in which a hormone diffuses from its cell of origin directly to target cells without entering the circulation, is known as paracrine function. Excellent examples of the paracrine actions of hormones are provided by the ovaries and testes. Estrogens produced in the ovaries are crucial for the maturation of ovarian follicles before ovulation. Similarly, testosterone produced by the Leydig cells of the testes acts on adjacent seminiferous tubules to stimulate spermatogenesis (the origin and development of sperm cells). In these instances, very high local concentrations of hormones stimulate the target organs. A hormone also may act on its own cell, a phenomenon known as autocrine function.

GLANDS AND HORMONES OF THE HUMAN ENDOCRINE SYSTEM		
GLAND OR TISSUE	PRINCIPAL HORMONE	FUNCTION
testis	testosterone	stimulates development of male sex organs and secondary sex characteristics, including facial hair growth and increased muscle mass
ovary	estrogens (estradiol, estrone, estriol)	stimulate development of female sex organs and secondary sex characteristics, maturation of ovarian follicles, formation and maintenance of bone tissue, and contraction of the uterine muscles

GLANDS AND HORMONES OF THE HUMAN ENDOCRINE SYSTEM

GLAND OR TISSUE	PRINCIPAL HORMONE	FUNCTION
	inhibin (folliculostin)	inhibits secretion of follicle-stimulating hormone from the pituitary gland
	progesterone	stimulates secretion of substances from the lining of the uterus (endometrium) in preparation for egg implantation in the uterine wall
	relaxin	induces relaxation of pubic ligaments during childbirth to facilitate infant delivery
thyroid gland	thyroxine	stimulates cellular metabolism, lipid production, carbohydrate utilization, and central and autonomic nervous system activation
	triiodothyronine	stimulates cellular metabolism, lipid production, carbohydrate utilization, and central and autonomic nervous system activation
adrenal gland, medulla	epinephrine (adrenaline)	stimulates "fight or flight" response, increases heart rate, dilates blood vessels in skeletal muscles and liver, increases oxygen delivery to muscle and brain tissues, increases blood glucose concentrations, and suppresses digestion
	norepinephrine (noradrenaline)	stimulates "fight or flight" response, increases heart rate, constricts blood vessels, increases blood glucose concentrations, and suppresses digestion

GLANDS AND HORMONES OF THE HUMAN ENDOCRINE SYSTEM

GLAND OR TISSUE	PRINCIPAL HORMONE	FUNCTION
adrenal gland, cortex	cortisol	activates physiological stress responses to maintain blood glucose concentrations, augments constriction of blood vessels to maintain blood pressure, and stimulates anti-inflammatory pathways
	aldosterone	regulates balance of salt and water in the body
	androgens	contribute to growth and development of the male reproductive system and serve as precursors to testosterone and estrogen
pituitary gland, anterior lobe	corticotropin (adrenocorticotropin, ACTH)	stimulates growth and secretion of cells of the adrenal cortex; increases skin pigmentation
	growth hormone (GH; somatotropin)	stimulates growth of essentially all tissues in the body
	thyrotropin (thyroid-stimulating hormone)	stimulates secretion of thyroid hormone and growth of thyroid cells
	follicle-stimulating hormone (FSH)	stimulates maturation of egg follicles in females and development of spermatozoa in males
	luteinizing hormone (LH; interstitial cell stimulating hormone, ICSH)	stimulates rupture of mature egg follicles and production of progesterone and androgens in females and secretion of androgens in males

GLANDS AND HORMONES OF THE HUMAN ENDOCRINE SYSTEM

GLAND OR TISSUE	PRINCIPAL HORMONE	FUNCTION
	prolactin (PRL; luteotropic hormone, LTH; lactogenic hormone; mammotropin	stimulates and maintains lactation in breast-feeding mothers
pituitary gland, posterior lobe	oxytocin	stimulates milk ejection during breast-feeding and uterine muscle contraction during childbirth
	vasopressin (antidiuretic hormone, ADH)	regulates fluid volume by increasing or decreasing fluid excretion in response to changes in blood pressure
pituitary gland, intermediate lobe	melanocyte-stimulating hormones (MSH)*	stimulate melanin synthesis in skin cells to increase skin pigmentation; may also suppress appetite
hypothalamus	corticotropin-releasing hormone (CRH)	stimulates synthesis and secretion of corticotropin from the anterior pituitary gland
	growth hormone-releasing hormone (GHRH)	stimulates synthesis and secretion of growth hormone from the anterior pituitary gland
	thyrotropin-releasing hormone (TRH)	stimulates and regulates secretion of thyrotropin from the anterior pituitary gland and may modulate neuronal activity in the brain and spinal cord

GLANDS AND HORMONES OF THE HUMAN ENDOCRINE SYSTEM

GLAND OR TISSUE	PRINCIPAL HORMONE	FUNCTION
	gonadotropin-releasing hormone (GnRH)	stimulates synthesis and secretion of follicle-stimulating hormone and luteinizing hormone from the anterior pituitary gland
	prolactin-inhibiting factor (PIF; dopamine)	inhibits secretion of prolactin from the anterior pituitary gland
	somatostatin	inhibits secretion of growth hormone from the anterior pituitary gland, inhibits secretion of insulin and glucagon in the pancreas, and inhibits secretion of gastrointestinal hormones and secretion of acid in the stomach
	gastrointestinal neuropeptides	hormones secreted from the stomach and pancreas that stimulate hypothalamic secretion of neuropeptides, such as neuropeptide Y, gastrin-releasing peptide, and somatostatin, that regulate appetite, fat storage, and metabolism
pancreatic islets of Langerhans	glucagon	maintains blood glucose concentrations by stimulating release of glucose from the liver and production of glucose from amino acids and glycerol
	insulin	stimulates glucose uptake and storage in adipose, muscle, and liver tissues

GLANDS AND HORMONES OF THE HUMAN ENDOCRINE SYSTEM

GLAND OR TISSUE	PRINCIPAL HORMONE	FUNCTION
	somatostatin	inhibits glucagon and insulin secretion from the pancreas and inhibits secretion of gastrointestinal hormones and secretion of acid in the stomach
	pancreatic polypeptide	inhibits contraction of the gallbladder and secretion of exocrine substances from the pancreas
parathyroid gland	parathyroid hormone (parathormone)	increases serum calcium concentrations by stimulating release of calcium from bone tissue, reabsorption of calcium in the kidneys, and production of vitamin D in the kidneys; inhibits reabsorption of phosphate in the kidneys
	calcitonin	decreases serum calcium concentrations by promoting uptake of calcium into bone tissue and excretion of calcium in the urine
skin, liver, kidneys	calciferols (vitamin D)	maintain serum calcium concentrations by increasing absorption of calcium and phosphate in the intestines and reabsorption of calcium and phosphate in the kidneys; mobilizes calcium from bone in response to parathyroid hormone activity
stomach	gastrin	stimulates secretion of acid and pepsin in the stomach and contraction of the pyloric region of the stomach near the small intestine to increase motility during digestion

GLANDS AND HORMONES OF THE HUMAN ENDOCRINE SYSTEM

GLAND OR TISSUE	PRINCIPAL HORMONE	FUNCTION
duodenum	cholecystokinin (CCK; pancreozymin)	stimulates release of bile from the gallbladder into the intestine and stimulates secretion of pancreatic juices into the intestine; may induce satiety
	secretin	stimulates secretion of water and bicarbonate from the pancreas into the duodenum; inhibits secretion of gastrin in the stomach, delaying gastric emptying
	gastric-inhibitory polypeptide (GIP)	inhibits secretion of acid into the stomach; stimulates secretion of insulin from the pancreas
	vasoactive intestinal peptide (VIP)	stimulates dilation of blood vessels and secretion of water and electrolytes from the intestine; modulates immune functions
pineal gland	melatonin	regulates circadian rhythm (primarily in response to light and dark cycles) and release of gonadotropin-releasing hormone from the hypothalamus and gonadotropins from the pituitary gland
kidneys	renin	regulates blood pressure and blood flow by catalyzing conversion of angiotensinogen to angiotensin I in the kidneys
multiple tissues	insulin-like growth factors (somatomedins)	stimulate growth by mediating secretion of growth hormone from the pituitary gland
	prostaglandins	regulate many physiological processes, including dilation and constriction of blood vessels, aggregation of platelets, and inflammation

*Intermediate lobe hormones referred to collectively as melanotropin or intermedin.

ADRENAL GLAND

The adrenal gland (sometimes called the suprarenal gland) is either of two small triangular endocrine glands that are located above each kidney. In humans each adrenal gland weighs about 5 grams (0.18 ounce) and measures about 30 mm (1.2 inches) wide, 50 mm (2 inches) long, and 10 mm (0.4 inch) thick. Each gland consists of two parts: an inner medulla, which produces the neurotransmitters epinephrine and norepinephrine (adrenaline and noradrenaline), and an outer cortex, which produces steroid hormones. The two parts differ in embryological origin, structure, and function. The adrenal glands vary in size, shape, and nerve supply in other animal species. In some vertebrates the cells of the two parts are interspersed to varying degrees.

ADRENAL MEDULLA

The adrenal medulla is embedded in the centre of the cortex of each adrenal gland. It is small, making up only about 10 percent of the total adrenal weight. The adrenal medulla is composed of chromaffin cells that are named for the granules within the cells that darken after exposure to chromium salts. These cells migrate to the adrenal medulla from the embryonic neural crest and represent specialized neural tissue. Indeed, the adrenal medulla is an integral part of the sympathetic nervous system, a major subdivision of the autonomic nervous system. The sympathetic nervous system and the adrenal medulla are collectively known as the sympathoadrenal system. The chromaffin granules contain the hormones of the adrenal medulla, which include dopamine, norepinephrine, and epinephrine. When stimulated by sympathetic nerve impulses, the chromaffin granules are released from the cells and the hormones enter the circulation, a process known as exocytosis. Thus, the adrenal medulla is a neurohemal organ (a neurohemal organ is one with structures that contain neurosecretory neurons).

ADRENAL CORTEX

Cells of the adrenal cortex synthesize and secrete chemical derivatives (steroids) of cholesterol. While cholesterol can be synthesized in many body tissues, further modification into steroid hormones takes place only in the adrenal cortex and its embryological cousins, the ovaries and the testes. In adult humans the outer cortex comprises about 90 percent of each adrenal gland. It is composed of three structurally different concentric zones. From the outside in, they are the zona glomerulosa, zona fasciculata, and zona reticularis.

The zona glomerulosa produces aldosterone, which acts on the kidneys to conserve salt and water. The inner two zones of the adrenal cortex—the zona fasciculata and the zona reticularis—function as a physiological unit to produce cortisol and adrenal androgens (male hormones), with dehydroepiandrosterone, a weak androgen, being the major product. Cortisol has two primary actions: (1) stimulation of gluconeogenesis—i.e., the breakdown of protein and fat in muscle and their conversion to glucose in the liver—and (2) anti-inflammatory actions. Cortisol and synthetic derivatives of it, such as prednisone and dexamethasone, are known as glucocorticoids, so named because of their ability to stimulate gluconeogenesis. In severely stressed patients these compounds not only facilitate glucose production but also raise blood pressure and reduce inflammation. Because of their anti-inflammatory properties, they are often given to patients with inflammatory diseases such as rheumatoid arthritis and asthma. Glucocorticoids also reduce the function and action of the immune system, making them useful for protecting against transplant rejection and ameliorating autoimmune and allergic diseases.

REGULATION OF ADRENAL HORMONE SECRETION

The secretion of cortisol and aldosterone is regulated by different mechanisms. The secretion of cortisol is regulated by the classical hypothalamic-pituitary-adrenal feedback system. The major determinant that controls the secretion of cortisol is adrenocorticotropin. In normal subjects there is both pulsatile and diurnal (referred to as a circadian rhythm) secretion of this hormone, which causes pulsatile and diurnal secretion of cortisol. Variations in the secretion of adrenocorticotropin are caused by variations in the secretion of corticotropin-releasing hormone by the hypothalamus and by variations in serum cortisol concentrations. An increase in serum cortisol concentrations inhibits the secretion of both corticotropin-releasing hormone and adrenocorticotropin. Conversely, a decrease in serum cortisol concentration results in an increase in the secretion of corticotropin-releasing hormone and adrenocorticotropin, thereby restoring the secretion of cortisol to normal concentrations. However, if the adrenal glands are unable to respond to stimulation by adrenocorticotropin, decreased serum cortisol concentrations will persist. Severe physical or emotional stresses stimulate the secretion of corticotropin-releasing hormone and adrenocorticotropin, resulting in large increases in serum cortisol concentrations. However, under these circumstances, increased serum cortisol concentrations do not inhibit the secretion of corticotropin-releasing hormone or adrenocorticotropin and thereby allow large amounts of cortisol to be secreted until the stress subsides. Adrenocorticotropin also stimulates the secretion of adrenal androgens from the adrenal cortex, but the androgens do not inhibit adrenocorticotropin secretion.

Aldosterone secretion is regulated primarily by the renin-angiotensin system. Renin is an enzyme secreted into the blood from specialized cells that encircle the arterioles (small arteries) at the entrance to the glomeruli of the kidneys (the renal capillary networks that are the filtration units of the kidney). The renin-secreting cells, which compose the juxtaglomerular apparatus, are sensitive to changes in blood flow and blood pressure, and the primary stimulus for increased renin secretion is decreased blood flow to the kidneys. A decrease in blood flow may be caused by loss of sodium and water (as a result of diarrhea, persistent vomiting, or excessive perspiration) or by narrowing of a renal artery. Renin catalyzes the conversion of a plasma protein called angiotensinogen into a decapeptide (consisting of 10 amino acids) called angiotensin I. An enzyme in the serum called angiotensin-converting enzyme (ACE) then converts angiotensin I into an octapeptide (consisting of eight amino acids) called angiotensin II. Angiotensin II acts via specific receptors in the adrenal glands to stimulate the secretion of aldosterone, which stimulates salt and water reabsorption by the kidneys, and the constriction of arterioles, which causes an increase in blood pressure. Aldosterone secretion is also stimulated by high serum potassium concentrations (hyperkalemia) and to a lesser extent by adrenocorticotropin. Excessive aldosterone production or excessive renin secretion, which leads to excessive angiotensin and aldosterone production, can cause high blood pressure.

HYPOTHALAMUS

The hypothalamus is the region of the brain lying below the thalamus and making up the floor of the third cerebral ventricle. The hypothalamus is an integral part of the brain. It is a small cone-shaped structure that projects downward from the brain, ending in the infundibular stalk (or stem), a tubular connection to the pituitary gland. The hypothalamus contains a control centre for many functions of the autonomic nervous system, and it has effects on the endocrine system because of its complex interaction with the pituitary gland.

ANATOMY OF THE HYPOTHALAMUS

The hypothalamus and pituitary gland are connected by both nervous and chemical pathways. The posterior portion of the hypothalamus, called the median eminence, contains the nerve endings of many neurosecretory cells, which run down through the infundibular stalk (or pituitary stalk) into the pituitary gland. Important structures adjacent to the median eminence of the hypothalamus include the mammillary bodies (a pair of tiny round structures on the underside of the brain), the third ventricle (or cavity), and the optic chiasm (a part of the visual system). Above the hypothalamus is the thalamus.

HYPOTHALAMIC REGULATION OF HORMONE SECRETION

The hypothalamus, like the rest of the brain, consists of interconnecting neurons that are nourished by a rich supply of blood. To understand hypothalamic function, it is necessary to define the various forms of neurosecretion. First, there is neurotransmission, which occurs throughout the brain and is the process by which one nerve cell communicates with another via a synapse between the ends (nerve terminals) of neurons. Nerve terminals are often called presynaptic or postsynaptic in reference to the direction in which an impulse is traveling, with the presynaptic neuron transmitting an impulse to the postsynaptic neuron.

Transmission of an electrical impulse requires the secretion of a chemical substance that diffuses across the synapse from the presynaptic membrane of one neuron to the postsynaptic membrane of another neuron. The chemical substance that is secreted is called a neurotransmitter. The process of synthesis and secretion of neurotransmitters is similar to that of protein hormone synthesis, with the exception that the neurotransmitters are contained within neurosecretory granules that are produced in the cell body and migrate through the axon (a projection of the neuron) to the nerve terminal, from which they are discharged into the synaptic space.

There are four classic neurotransmitters: epinephrine, norepinephrine, serotonin, and acetylcholine. A large number of additional neurotransmitters have been discovered, of which an important group is the neuropeptides. The neuropeptides function not only as neurotransmitters but also as neuromodulators. As neuromodulators, they do not act directly as neurotransmitters but rather increase or decrease the action of neurotransmitters. Well-known examples are the opioids (e.g., enkephalins), which are endogenous (produced in the human body) peptides with a strong affinity for the receptors that bind opiate drugs, such as morphine and heroin.

The brain and indeed the entire central nervous system consist of an interconnected network of neurons. The secretion of specific neurotransmitters and neuropeptides lends an organized, directed function to the overall system. The connection of the hypothalamus to many other regions of the brain, including the cerebral cortex, allows intellectual and functional signals, as well as external signals, including physical and emotional stresses, to be funneled into the hypothalamus to the endocrine system. From the endocrine system these signals are able to exert their effects throughout the body.

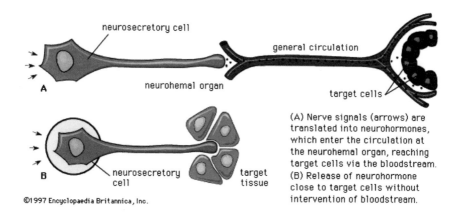

(A) Nerve signals (arrows) are translated into neurohormones, which enter the circulation at the neurohemal organ, reaching target cells via the bloodstream. (B) Release of neurohormone close to target cells without intervention of bloodstream.

©1997 Encyclopaedia Britannica, Inc.

Neurohormones are released from neurosecretory nerve cells. These nerve cells are considered true endocrine cells because they produce and secrete hormones that enter the circulation to reach their target cells.

The hypothalamus produces and secretes not only neurotransmitters and neuropeptides but also several neurohormones that alter anterior pituitary gland function and two hormones, vasopressin and oxytocin, that act on distant target organs. The neurons that produce and secrete neurohormones are true endocrine cells in that they produce hormones that are incorporated into secretory granules that are then carried through the axons and stored in nerve terminals located in the median eminence or posterior pituitary gland. In response to neural stimuli, the contents of the secretory granules are extruded from the nerve terminals into a capillary network. In the case of hormones that affect pituitary function, the contents of the secretory granules are carried through the hypophyseal-portal circulation and are delivered directly into the anterior pituitary gland.

These hypothalamic neurohormones are known as releasing hormones because their major function is to stimulate the secretion of hormones originating in the anterior pituitary gland. For example, certain releasing hormones secreted from the hypothalamus trigger the release from the anterior pituitary of substances such as adrenocorticotropin and luteinizing hormone. The hypothalamic neurohormones consist of simple peptides ranging in size from only 3 amino acids (thyrotropin-releasing hormone) to 44 amino acids (growth hormone-releasing hormone). One hypothalamic hormone, somatostatin, has an inhibitory action, primarily inhibiting the secretion of growth hormone although it can also inhibit the secretion of other hormones. The neurotransmitter dopamine, produced in the hypothalamus and in small amounts in the adrenal medulla, also has an inhibitory action, inhibiting the secretion of the anterior pituitary hormone prolactin. The cell bodies of the neurons that produce these neurohormones are not evenly distributed throughout the hypothalamus. Instead, they are grouped together in paired clusters of cell bodies known as nuclei.

A classic model for neurohormonal activity is the posterior lobe of the pituitary gland (the neurohypophysis). Its secretory products, vasopressin and oxytocin, are produced and packaged into neurosecretory granules in specific groups of nerve cells in the hypothalamus (the supraoptic nuclei and the paraventricular nuclei). The granules are carried through the axons that extend through the infundibular stalk and end in and form the posterior lobe of the pituitary gland. In response to nerve signals, the secretory granules are extruded into a capillary network that feeds directly into the general circulation.

In addition to regulating the release of pituitary hormones, the hypothalamus also influences caloric intake and weight regulation, establishing a stable "set point" for individual weight gain. The hypothalamus also regulates body heat in response to variations in external temperature, determines wakefulness and sleep, and regulates fluid intake and sensation of thirst.

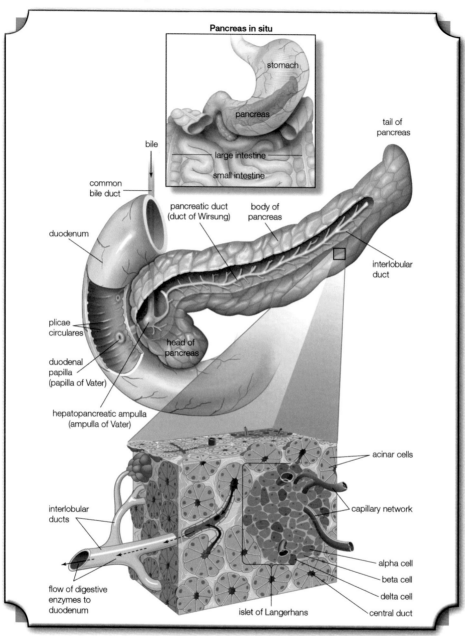

Pancreas in situ

stomach

pancreas

large intestine

small intestine

tail of pancreas

bile

common bile duct

pancreatic duct (duct of Wirsung)

body of pancreas

duodenum

interlobular duct

plicae circulares

head of pancreas

duodenal papilla (papilla of Vater)

hepatopancreatic ampulla (ampulla of Vater)

acinar cells

interlobular ducts

capillary network

alpha cell

beta cell

delta cell

flow of digestive enzymes to duodenum

islet of Langerhans

central duct

The islets of Langerhans are responsible for the endocrine function of the pancreas. Each islet contains beta, alpha, and delta cells that are responsible for the secretion of pancreatic hormones. Beta cells secrete insulin, a well-characterized hormone that plays an important role in regulating glucose metabolism. Encyclopædia Britannica, Inc.

ISLETS OF LANGERHANS

The islets, or islands, of Langerhans are irregularly shaped patches of endocrine tissue located within the pancreas of most vertebrates. They are named for the German physician Paul Langerhans, who first described them in 1869. The normal human pancreas contains about 1,000,000 islets. The islets consist of four distinct cell types, of which three (alpha, beta, and delta cells) produce important hormones. The fourth component (C cells) has no known function.

The most common islet cell, the beta cell, produces insulin, the major hormone in the regulation of carbohydrate, fat, and protein metabolism. Insulin is crucial in several metabolic processes: it promotes the uptake and metabolism of glucose by the body's cells, and it prevents release of glucose by the liver. It also causes muscle cells to take up amino acids, the basic components of protein, and it inhibits the breakdown and release of fats. The release

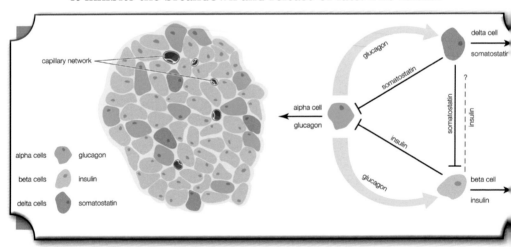

The islets of Langerhans contain alpha, beta, and delta cells that produce glucagon, insulin, and somatostatin, respectively. A fourth type of islet cell, the F (or PP) cell, is located at the periphery of the islets and secretes pancreatic polypeptide. These hormones regulate one another's secretion through paracrine cell-cell interactions. Encyclopædia Britannica, Inc.

of insulin from the beta cells can be triggered by growth hormone or by glucagon, but the most important stimulator of insulin release is glucose. When the blood glucose level increases—as it does after a meal—insulin is released to counter it. The inability of the islet cells to make insulin or the failure to produce amounts sufficient to control blood glucose level are the causes of diabetes mellitus.

The alpha cells of the islets of Langerhans produce an opposing hormone, glucagon, which releases glucose from the liver and fatty acids from fat tissue. In turn, glucose and free fatty acids favour insulin release and inhibit glucagon release. The delta cells produce somatostatin, a strong inhibitor of growth hormone, insulin, and glucagon.

OVARIES

The ovaries are the female reproductive organs that produce eggs and the female sex hormones estrogen and progesterone. Human females have two ovaries, each of which is almond-shaped and is about 4 cm (1.6 inches) long, 2 cm (0.8 inch) wide, and 1.5 cm (0.6 inch) thick.

Each ovary contains hollow balls of cells (follicles) that hold immature eggs. About 150,000–500,000 follicles usually are present at birth, but by young adulthood, only about 34,000 remain. The number continues to decrease until menopause (the cessation of ovarian function), when the few remaining follicles decay and the ovaries shrink and produce far less estrogen. Only 300–400 follicles mature and release an egg, which develops into an embryo if fertilized by a male's sperm or, if not, passes from the body with menstruation (periodic discharge of the uterine lining).

Because the ovaries secrete both estrogen and progesterone into the bloodstream, they are important endocrine glands. Before the onset of puberty the ovaries are quiescent, and the cortex of each ovary contains only immature follicles. Puberty begins with pulsatile noctur-nal secretion of gonadotropin-releasing hormone (GnRH) from the hypothalamus. Nocturnal pulses are initiated at least in part by increasing body size, which may cause an increase in the secretion of leptin (from the Greek *leptos*, meaning "thin"; a protein hormone impor-tant for regulation of reproduction, metabolism, and body weight), which in turn stimulates the secretion of GnRH. Pulsatile secretion of GnRH activates the gonad-otroph cells of the anterior pituitary, resulting in pulses of secretion of moderate quantities of FSH (follicle-stim-ulating hormone) and of significant quantities of LH (luteinizing hormone). In time, pulsatile secretion of GnRH and pulsatile secretion of the gonadotropins occur continuously. Increasing secretion of gonadotro-pins leads to increasing production of estrogens by the ovaries. Estrogens stimulate the development of second-ary sex characteristics and the maturation of ovarian follicles. Increased secretion of estrogens normally occurs between ages 8 and 14 in girls.

With continued maturation of the hypothalamus, pitu-itary, and ovaries, the cyclic hypothalamic-pituitary-ovarian activity characteristic of adult women begins. During the first days of the menstrual cycle, secretion of FSH increases, causing the maturation of follicles as described above. As follicles mature, they secrete more estradiol (the most potent of the estrogens), which is paralleled by an increase in the secretion of LH. Increased secretion of LH stimu-lates the secretion of more estradiol and a small amount of progesterone that then trigger a transient surge in LH secretion and to a lesser extent FSH secretion, causing rup-ture of the mature Graafian follicle. The surge in LH secretion can be readily detected in the urine, providing a means whereby women can determine if they have ovu-lated and therefore are potentially fertile.

The follicular phase of the cycle ends at the time of ovulation. Serum LH, FSH, and estradiol concentrations then decrease considerably, and the corpus luteum begins to produce some estrogen and large quantities of progesterone. This is known as the luteal phase of the menstrual cycle, which lasts until the corpus luteum degenerates (luteolysis) and estradiol and progesterone production decreases. The decreasing serum estrogen and progesterone concentrations result in constriction of uterine arteries, thus interrupting the delivery of oxygen and nutrients to the endometrium. The endometrium is then sloughed off, causing the vaginal bleeding characteristic of menstruation. A new menstrual cycle then begins.

The normal menstrual cycle is typically divided into a follicular phase of about 14 days, during which the endometrium proliferates, and a luteal phase of about 14 days, which culminates with the endometrial lining being sloughed off. Thus, the two phases are separated by ovulation on the one hand and by menstruation on the other hand. The phases vary in length by several days in different women and sometimes in the same woman. Variations in cycle length are most common in the first years after menarche (the first menstrual cycle) and just before menopause (when menstruation ceases).

The changing serum estrogen and progesterone concentrations during the menstrual cycle have several other effects. Basal body temperature fluctuates little during the follicular phase of the menstrual cycle but increases abruptly after ovulation. This increase parallels the postovulatory increase in serum progesterone concentrations and is caused by an effect of progesterone on the temperature-regulating centres in the brain. The decrease in serum estradiol and progesterone concentrations near the end of the cycle may be accompanied by changes in mood and activity and by an increase in fluid retention. The changes initiated by the decrease in secretion of estradiol and progesterone comprise the symptoms of premenstrual syndrome, although the relationship between hormonal changes and these symptoms is unclear.

After menopause, the ovaries shrink in size and usually consist of old fibrous tissue. The production of estrogen drops considerably but does not totally cease.

PARATHYROID GLAND

The parathyroid gland is an endocrine gland located close to and behind the thyroid gland. Humans usually have four parathyroid glands, each composed of closely packed epithelial cells separated by thin fibrous bands and some fat cells. The parathyroid glands secrete parathormone (or parathyroid hormone), which functions to maintain normal serum calcium and phosphate concentrations.

ANATOMY OF THE PARATHYROID GLANDS

The parathyroid glands are small structures adjacent to or occasionally embedded in the thyroid gland. Each gland weighs about 50 mg (0.002 ounce). Because of their small size and their close association with the thyroid gland, it is not surprising that they were recognized as distinct endocrine organs rather late in the history of endocrinology. At the beginning of the 20th century, symptoms due to deficiency of the parathyroid glands were attributed to the absence of the thyroid gland. At that time, surgeons inadvertently removed the parathyroid glands when they removed the thyroid gland. It was recognized in the early part of the 20th century that parathyroid deficiency could be mitigated by the administration of calcium salts. Soon after, scientists successfully prepared active extracts of the parathyroid glands and characterized the parathyroid glands as endocrine glands that secreted parathormone. These discoveries were followed by the realization that parathyroid tumours caused high serum calcium concentrations.

FUNCTIONS OF THE PARATHYROID GLANDS

The major regulators of serum calcium concentrations are parathormone and the active metabolites of vitamin D (which facilitate calcium absorption from the gastrointestinal tract). A slight fall in serum calcium is enough to trigger parathormone secretion from the parathyroid cells, and chronically low serum calcium concentrations, which occur as a result of conditions such as vitamin D deficiency and kidney failure, cause abnormal increases in parathormone secretion. Increased parathormone secretion raises serum calcium levels by stimulating retention of calcium by the kidneys, mobilization of calcium from bone, and absorption of calcium by the gastrointestinal tract. Conversely, parathormone secretion is inhibited when serum calcium concentrations are high—for example, in vitamin D poisoning or in diseases that increase breakdown of bone (notably some cancers).

Low serum calcium concentrations (hypocalcemia) result in increased excitability of nerves and muscles (tetany), which causes muscle spasms, numbness and tingling around the mouth and in the hands and feet, and, occasionally, convulsions. High serum calcium concentrations (hypercalcemia) result in loss of appetite, nausea, vomiting, constipation, muscle weakness, fatigue, mental dysfunction, and increased thirst and urination.

Parathormone also affects the metabolism of phosphate. An excess of the hormone causes an increase in phosphate excretion in the urine and low serum phosphate concentrations. Reduced parathyroid function results in a decrease in phosphate excretion in the urine and high serum phosphate concentrations.

Parathormone also plays a role in the regulation of magnesium metabolism by increasing its excretion. Magnesium deficiency results in a decrease in parathormone secretion in some patients and decreased tissue action of parathormone in other patients.

PINEAL GLAND

The pineal gland is the source of the hormone melatonin. The pineal gland develops from the roof of the diencephalon, a section of the brain. In some lower vertebrates the gland has a well-developed eyelike structure. In others, though not organized as an eye, it functions as a light receptor.

The pineal gland, the most enigmatic of endocrine organs, has long been of interest to anatomists. Several millennia ago it was thought to control the flow of memories into consciousness. The 17th-century French philosopher-mathematician René Descartes concluded that the pineal gland was the seat of the soul. A corollary notion was that calcification of the pineal caused psychiatric disease, but modern imaging techniques revealed that the pineal gland becomes more or less calcified in most people.

ANATOMY OF THE PINEAL GLAND

The pineal gland is located behind the third cerebral ventricle in the midline (between the two cerebral hemispheres) of the brain. Its name is derived from its shape, which is like that of a pine cone (Latin *pinea*). In adult humans it is about 0.8 cm (0.3 inch) long and weighs

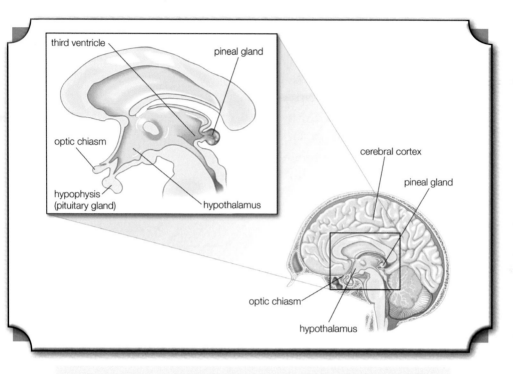

The human pineal gland is located behind the third cerebral ventricle in the midline (between the two cerebral hemispheres) of the brain. Encyclopædia Britannica, Inc.

approximately 0.1 gram (0.004 ounce). The gland is relatively large in children and begins to shrink with the onset of puberty. It has a rich supply of adrenergic nerves that greatly influence its function. Microscopically, the gland is composed of pinealocytes (rather typical endocrine cells except for extensions that mingle with those of adjacent cells) and supporting cells that are similar to the astrocytes of the brain. In adults, small deposits of calcium often make the pineal body visible on X-rays.

Endocrine Function of the Pineal Gland

In humans and other animals, the pineal gland produces hormones that have important endocrine functions. For example, in several vertebrate species, pineal hormones influence sexual development, hibernation, and seasonal breeding. The pineal gland contains several neuropeptides and neurotransmitters, such as somatostatin, norepinephrine, and serotonin. The major pineal hormone, however, is melatonin, a derivative of the amino acid tryptophan. Melatonin was first discovered because it lightens amphibian skin, an effect opposite to that of adrenocorticotropin and melanocyte-stimulating hormone of the anterior pituitary gland.

The secretion of melatonin is increased by sympathetic nervous system stimulation. In humans, melatonin secretion increases soon after a person is placed in the dark and decreases soon after exposure to light. A major action of melatonin that has been well documented in animals is to block the secretion of gonadotropin-releasing hormone by the hypothalamus. This results in decreased secretion of gonadotropins (e.g., LH and FSH) by the pituitary gland. In humans, however, the function of melatonin is less well understood. Its production is high in infancy and childhood and declines with age, and abnormally high levels of melatonin in children are associated with delayed sexual development.

PITUITARY GLAND

The pituitary gland (or hypophysis) is a ductless gland of the endocrine system that secretes hormones directly into the bloodstream. The term *hypophysis* (from the Greek for "lying under") refers to the gland's position on the underside of the brain. The pituitary gland has a major role in the regulation of many endocrine functions.

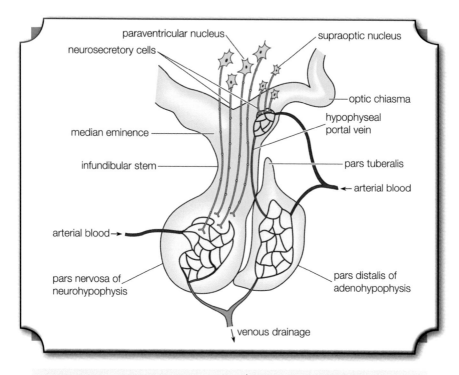

The anatomy of the mammalian pituitary gland, showing the anterior lobe (adenohypophysis), the posterior lobe (neurohypophysis), the paraventricular and supraoptic nuclei, and other major structures.
Encyclopædia Britannica, Inc.

ANATOMY OF THE PITUITARY GLAND

The pituitary gland lies at the base of the skull and is housed within a bony structure called the sella turcica. Its weight in normal adult humans is about 500 mg (0.02 ounce). The gland is attached to the hypothalamus by the pituitary stalk, which is composed of the axons of neurons and the hypophyseal-portal veins. In most species the pituitary gland is divided into three lobes: the anterior lobe, the intermediate lobe, and the posterior lobe. In humans the intermediate lobe does not exist as a distinct anatomic structure but rather remains only as cells dispersed within the anterior lobe. Despite its proximity to the anterior lobe of the pituitary, the posterior lobe of the pituitary is functionally distinct and is an integral part of a separate neural structure called the neurohypophysis.

THE ANTERIOR PITUITARY

The cells constituting the anterior lobe of the pituitary gland are embryologically derived from an outpouching of the roof of the pharynx, known as Rathke's pouch. While the cells appear to be relatively homogeneous under a light microscope, there are in fact five different types of cells, each of which secretes a different hormone or hormones. The thyrotrophs synthesize and secrete thyrotropin; the gonadotrophs, both LH and FSH; the corticotrophs, adrenocorticotropin; the somatotrophs, growth hormone; and the lactotrophs, prolactin.

Somatotrophs are plentiful in the anterior pituitary gland, constituting about 40 percent of the tissue. They are located predominantly in the anterior and the lateral regions of the gland and secrete between one and two milligrams of growth hormone each day.

STRUCTURE AND FUNCTION OF ANTERIOR PITUITARY HORMONES

Each pituitary hormone plays a vital role in endocrine function. The hormones of the anterior pituitary are proteins that consist of one or two long polypeptide chains. The gonadotropins (LH and FSH) and thyrotropin are called glycoproteins because they contain complex carbohydrates known as glycosides. Each of these three hormones—LH, FSH, and thyrotropin—is composed of two glycopeptide chains, one of which, the alpha chain, is identical in all three hormones. The other chain, the beta chain, differs in structure for each hormone, thereby explaining the different actions of each of these three hormones. As is the case for all protein hormones, the hormones of the anterior pituitary are synthesized in the cytoplasm of the cells as large, inactive molecules called prohormones. These prohormones are stored in granules, within which they are cleaved into active hormones and are secreted into the circulation.

REGULATION OF ANTERIOR PITUITARY HORMONES

The production of the anterior pituitary hormones is regulated in part by hormones produced in the hypothalamus. In general, hypothalamic hormones stimulate production of pituitary hormones, except for prolactin, which is inhibited. The hypothalamic hormones are secreted into a portal vein that traverses directly from the hypothalamus to the anterior pituitary gland, thereby carrying these hormones directly to the pituitary.

The posterior lobe is composed of the endings of nerve cells located in specialized regions of the hypothalamus. These nerve cells produce two hormones, oxytocin and vasopressin, that are carried down the nerves and stored in the nerve endings that compose the posterior pituitary gland. The hormones are released into the circulation in response to nerve signals that originate in the hypothalamus and are transmitted to the posterior pituitary. Oxytocin causes contraction of the uterus and milk secretion in women, and vasopressin increases reabsorption of water from the kidneys and raises blood pressure.

NEUROHYPOPHYSEAL SYSTEM

The posterior lobe of the pituitary gland consists largely of extensions of processes (axons) from two pairs of large clusters of nerve cell bodies (nuclei) in the hypothalamus. One of these nuclei, known as the supraoptic nuclei, lies immediately above the optic tract, while the other nuclei, known as the paraventricular nuclei, lies on each side of the third ventricle of the brain. These nuclei, the axons of the cell bodies of nerves that form the nuclei, and the nerve endings in the posterior pituitary gland form the neurohypophyseal system. There are neural connections to the brain and other centres of the hypothalamus, including a centre that modulates thirst.

The two neurohypophyseal hormones, vasopressin and oxytocin, are synthesized and incorporated into neurosecretory granules in the cell bodies of the nuclei. These hormones are synthesized as part of a precursor protein that includes one of the hormones and a protein called neurophysin. After synthesis and incorporation into neurosecretory granules, the precursor protein is cleaved, forming separate hormone and neurophysin molecules, which remain loosely attached to one another. These granules are carried through the axons and are stored in the posterior lobe of the pituitary gland. Upon stimulation of the nerve cells, the granules fuse with the cell wall of the nerve endings, the hormone and neurophysin dissociate from one another, and both the hormone and the neurophysin are released into the bloodstream.

TESTES

The testes are the male reproductive organs. Human males have two oval-shaped testes, measuring about 4–5 cm (1.5–2 inches) in length. These organs produce sperm and androgens (male hormones) and are contained in a sac (scrotum) behind the penis. Each testis is divided into 200–400 lobes and contains 3–10 very thin coiled tubes (seminiferous tubules), which produce sperm and which contract to expel the sperm through a complex network of canals to another structure in the scrotum, the epididymis, for temporary storage. The sperm cells in the testes are undeveloped in early childhood. At puberty, however, they are stimulated by hormones to develop into fertile sperm cells.

The principal androgen produced by the testes is testosterone. The production of testosterone by the testes is stimulated by LH, which is produced by the anterior pituitary and acts via receptors on the surface of the Leydig cells. The secretion of LH is stimulated by gonadotropin-releasing hormone (GnRH), which is released from the hypothalamus, and is inhibited by testosterone, which also inhibits the secretion of GnRH. These hormones constitute the hypothalamic-pituitary-testes axis. When serum testosterone concentrations decrease, the secretion of GnRH and LH increase. In contrast, when serum testosterone concentrations increase, the secretion of GnRH and LH decrease. These mechanisms maintain serum testosterone concentrations within a narrow range. In addition, the secretion of GnRH and the secretion of LH must be pulsatile to maintain normal testosterone production. Continuous administration of GnRH results in a decrease in the secretion of LH and therefore a decrease in the secretion of testosterone.

In boys as in girls, puberty begins with the onset of nocturnal pulses of GnRH, which stimulate pulses of FSH and LH. The testes enlarge and begin to secrete testosterone, which then stimulates the development of male secondary sex characteristics, including facial, axillary, pubic, and truncal hair growth; scrotal pigmentation;

prostatic enlargement; increased muscle mass and strength; increased libido; and increased linear growth. Many boys also have transient breast enlargement (gynecomastia) during puberty. This process starts at age 10 or 11 and is complete between ages 16 and 18.

Testosterone produced locally in the testes and FSH produced distally in the pituitary gland stimulate the process of spermatogenesis. Testosterone inhibits the secretion of FSH, which is also inhibited by inhibin, a polypeptide hormone produced by the Sertoli cells. Testosterone production and spermatogenesis decrease very slowly in older men—in contrast to women, whose ovarian function ceases abruptly at the time of menopause.

THYROID GLAND

The thyroid gland is located in the anterior (front) part of the lower neck, below the larynx (voice box). It secretes hormones vital to metabolism and growth.

ANATOMY OF THE THYROID GLAND

The thyroid arises from a downward outpouching of the floor of the pharynx, and a persisting remnant of this migration is known as a thyroglossal duct. The gland itself consists of two oblong lobes lying on either side of the trachea (windpipe) and connected by a narrow band of tissue called the isthmus. In normal adults the thyroid gland weighs 10 to 15 grams (0.4 to 0.5 ounce), though it has the capacity to grow much larger.

The lobes of the gland, as well as the isthmus, contain many small globular sacs called follicles. The follicles are lined with follicular cells and are filled with a fluid known as colloid that contains the prohormone thyroglobulin.

Thyroid gland

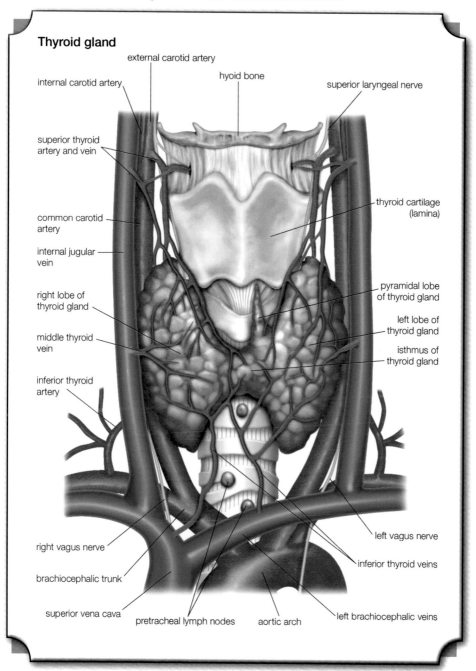

The human thyroid gland. Its two lobes are connected by an isthmus resembling the letter H. © Encyclopædia Britannica, Inc.

The follicular cells contain the enzymes needed to synthesize thyroglobulin, as well as the enzymes needed to release thyroid hormone from thyroglobulin. When thyroid hormones are needed, thyroglobulin is reabsorbed from the colloid in the follicular lumen into the cells, where it is split into its component parts, including the two thyroid hormones thyroxine (T_4) and triiodothyronine (T_3). The hormones are then released, passing from the cells into the circulation.

BIOCHEMISTRY OF THYROID HORMONE

Thyroxine and triiodothyronine contain iodine and are formed from thyronines, which are composed of two molecules of the amino acid tyrosine. (Both iodine and tyrosine are acquired in the diet.) Thyroxine contains four iodine atoms, and triiodothyronine contains three iodine atoms. Because each molecule of tyrosine binds one or two iodine atoms, two tyrosines are used to synthesize both thyroxine and triiodothyronine. These two hormones are the only biologically active substances that contain iodine, and they cannot be produced in the absence of iodine. The process leading to the eventual synthesis of thyroxine and triiodothyronine begins in the thyroid follicular cells, which concentrate iodine from the serum. The iodine is then oxidized and attached to tyrosine residues (forming compounds called iodotyrosines) within thyroglobulin molecules. The iodinated tyrosine residues are then rearranged to form thyroxine and triiodothyronine. Therefore, thyroglobulin serves not only as the structure within which thyroxine and triiodothyronine are synthesized but also as the storage form of the two hormones.

Considerably more thyroxine is produced and secreted by the thyroid gland than is triiodothyronine. However, thyronine

3,5,3′,5′-tetraiodothyronine (T₄)
(thyroxine)

3,5,3′-triiodothyronine (T₃)

3,3′,5′-triiodothyronine
(reverse T₃; rT₃)

Structural drawing of T_3, reverse T_3, and T_4, showing the synthesis of T_3 and reverse T_3 from T_4. ENCYCLOPÆDIA BRITANNICA, INC.

thyroxine is converted to triiodothyronine in many tissues by the action of enzymes called deiodinases. After thyroxine enters a cell, deiodinases located in the cytoplasm remove one of its four iodine atoms, converting it into triiodothyronine. The triiodothyronine either enters the nucleus of the cell or is returned to the circulation. As a result, all of the thyroxine and about 20 percent of the triiodothyronine produced each day come from the thyroid gland. The remaining 80 percent of triiodothyronine comes from deiodination of thyroxine outside of the thyroid. Most if not all of the action of thyroid hormone in its target tissues is exerted by triiodothyronine. Therefore, thyroxine may be considered a circulating precursor of triiodothyronine.

In serum more than 99 percent of the thyroxine and triiodothyronine is bound to one of three proteins. These binding proteins are known as thyroxine-binding globulin, transthyretin (thyroxine-binding prealbumin), and albumin. The remaining thyroxine and triiodothyronine (less than 1 percent) is free, or unbound. When free hormone enters a cell, it is replenished immediately by hormone attached to the binding proteins. The binding proteins serve as reservoirs of the two hormones to protect the tissues from sudden surges of thyroid hormone production and probably also to facilitate delivery of the hormones to the cells of large, solid organs such as the liver.

Essentially all cells in the body are target cells of triiodothyronine. Once triiodothyronine is inside a cell, it enters the nucleus, where it binds to proteins known as nuclear receptors. The triiodothyronine-receptor complexes then bind to deoxyribonucleic acid (DNA) molecules. This results in an increase in the rate at which the affected DNA molecules are transcribed to produce messenger ribonucleic acid (mRNA) molecules and an increase in the rate of synthesis of the protein (translation) coded for by the DNA (by way of the mRNA). Triiodothyronine increases the transcription of DNA molecules that code for many different proteins. However, it also inhibits the transcription of DNA that codes for certain other proteins. The patterns of activation and inhibition differ in different tissue and cell types.

ACTIONS OF THYROID HORMONE

The substances produced in increased quantities in response to triiodothyronine secretion include many enzymes, cell constituents, and hormones. Key among them are proteins that regulate the utilization of nutrients and the consumption of oxygen by the mitochondria of cells. Mitochondria are the sites at which energy in the form of adenosine triphosphate (ATP) is produced or is dissipated in the form of heat. Triiodothyronine activates substances that increase the proportion of energy that is dissipated as heat. It also stimulates carbohydrate utilization, lipid production and metabolism (thereby increasing cholesterol utilization), and central and autonomic nervous system activation, resulting in increased contraction of cardiac muscle and increased heart rate. During fetal life and in infancy this stimulatory activity of triiodothyronine is critically important for normal neural and skeletal growth and development. In both the unborn and the newborn, thyroid deficiency is associated with dwarfism and intellectual disability.

REGULATION OF THYROID HORMONE SECRETION

The thyroid gland is one component of the hypothalamic-pituitary-thyroid axis, which is a prime example of a negative feedback control system. The production and secretion of thyroxine and triiodothyronine by the thyroid gland are stimulated by the hypothalamic hormone thyrotropin-releasing hormone and the anterior pituitary hormone thyrotropin. In turn, the thyroid hormones inhibit the production and secretion of both thyrotropin-releasing hormone and thyrotropin. Decreased production of thyroid hormone results in increased thyrotropin secretion and thus increased thyroid hormone secretion. This restores serum thyroid hormone concentrations to normal levels. Conversely, increased production of thyroid hormone or administration of high doses of thyroid hormone inhibit the secretion of thyrotropin. As a result of this inhibition, serum thyroid hormone concentrations are able to fall toward normal levels. The complex interactions between thyroid hormone and thyrotropin maintain serum thyroid hormone concentrations within narrow limits. However, if the thyroid gland is severely damaged or if there is excessive thyroid hormone production independent of thyrotropin stimulation, hypothyroidism or hyperthyroidism ensues.

As already noted, much of the triiodothyronine produced each day is produced by deiodination of thyroxine in extrathyroidal tissues. The conversion of thyroxine to triiodothyronine significantly decreases in response to many adverse conditions, such as malnutrition, injury, or illness (including infections, cancer, and liver, heart, and kidney diseases). The production of triiodothyronine is also inhibited by starvation and by several drugs, notably amiodarone, a drug used to treat patients with cardiac rhythm disorders. In each of these situations, serum and tissue triiodothyronine concentrations decrease. This decrease in triiodothyronine production may be a beneficial adaptation to starvation and illness because it reduces the breakdown of protein and slows the use of nutrients for generating heat, thereby maintaining tissue integrity and conserving energy resources.

The fetal thyroid gland begins to function at about 12 weeks of gestation, and its function increases progressively thereafter. Within minutes after birth there is a sudden surge in thyrotropin secretion, followed by a marked increase in serum thyroxine and triiodothyronine concentrations. The concentrations of thyroid hormones then gradually decline, reaching adult values at the time of puberty. Thyroid hormone secretion increases in pregnant women. Therefore, women with thyroid deficiency who become pregnant usually need higher doses of thyroid hormone than when they are not pregnant. There is little change in thyroid secretion in older adults as compared with younger adults.

The Thyroid Gland and Calcitonin

The thyroid gland is also the site of the production of calcitonin, a hormone that can lower serum calcium concentrations by inhibiting the resorption of bone. The parafollicular (C) cells that produce calcitonin arise separately from the thyroid and migrate into it during development of the embryo. The C cells end up nestled in the spaces between the follicles. Because these cells have a separate embryological origin from the thyroid follicular cells, and because they secrete calcitonin, they in essence form a separate endocrine organ.

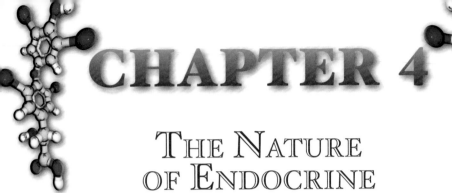

CHAPTER 4

THE NATURE OF ENDOCRINE DYSFUNCTION

There are a number of diseases and disorders that can disrupt endocrine function, and in many instances these conditions manifest as the overproduction or underproduction of hormone. Thus, the nature of endocrine dysfunction can be described in terms of hypofunction, when the production of a hormone is decreased, and hyperfunction, when the production of a hormone is increased. Although such changes in endocrine function arise from a diverse array of conditions, including glandular injury or an inherited endocrine disorder, there are normal physiological instances when hormone production is altered, although this is usually only temporary. Because many different hormones and glands contribute to normal endocrine function, endocrine hypofunction and hyperfunction often have not only direct effects on the hormone-producing gland but also secondary effects on target tissues.

ENDOCRINE HYPOFUNCTION AND RECEPTOR DEFECTS

In some cases, a decrease in hormone production, known as hypofunction, is required to maintain homeostasis. One example of hypofunction is decreased production of thyroid hormones during starvation and illness. Because the thyroid hormones control energy expenditure, there is survival value in slowing the body's metabolism when food intake is low. Thus, there is a distinction between compensatory endocrine hypofunction and true endocrine hypofunction.

ACQUIRED AND CONGENITAL ENDOCRINE HYPOFUNCTION

Endocrine glands may be destroyed in a variety of ways, but complete destruction is unusual. For most endocrine glands, at least 90 percent of the gland must be destroyed before major signs of hormone deficiency become apparent. There are many acquired causes of endocrine hypofunction. In the case of paired endocrine glands, such as the adrenal glands and the gonads, the removal of one of the pair is followed by a compensatory increase in the activity and the size of the remaining gland, which allows normal hormone levels to be maintained. In the case of physical trauma, including surgical trauma and severe hemorrhage within the gland, gland destruction may occur, which leads to endocrine hypofunction. Other acquired causes of endocrine hypofunction include infiltration by cancer cells or inflammatory cells; accumulation of large amounts of a metal (e.g., iron) or an abnormal protein (e.g., amyloid); bacterial, fungal, and viral infections; and damage from X-rays or radioactive elements.

Congenital defects or deficiencies can also cause endocrine gland hypofunction. Congenital endocrine gland hypofunction may be due to incomplete endocrine gland formation during fetal development or an inherited genetic mutation that causes deficiency of an enzyme needed for hormone synthesis, deficiency of substances needed for hormone production, or deficiency of receptors on target organs that leads to reduced hormonal action. In addition, congenital endocrine gland hypofunction may be caused by drugs or other substances that are

Following the March 2011 earthquake and tsunami in Japan, fear of radiation from the damaged Fukushima nuclear power plant hit the country. Here, an official in a radiation protection suit scans an evacuated woman with a Geiger counter at a shelter roughly 60 km (40 miles) west of the damaged plant. AFP/Getty Images

absorbed through the placenta, thereby blocking fetal hormone production and maternal hormone signaling. Since these disorders affect the primary source of particular hormones, they result in a set of conditions designated as primary endocrine gland hypofunction.

AUTOIMMUNE ENDOCRINE HYPOFUNCTION

Perhaps the single most common cause of endocrine hypofunction is autoimmunity. In autoimmune disorders, immune cells such as lymphocytes function improperly, producing antibodies that react with the body's own tissues instead of with foreign substances. In the endocrine system, autoimmune components act on and usually alter an endocrine gland's function. For instance, in the case of the thyroid gland, antibodies may be cytotoxic (cell-killing), damaging and eventually destroying the thyroid cells. In other cases, thyroid antibodies may be inhibitory, blocking the binding of thyrotropin to its receptors on thyroid cells and preventing the action of thyrotropin. In still other cases, thyroid antibodies may be stimulatory, mimicking the action of thyrotropin and causing thyroid hyperfunction. In some situations, cytotoxic lymphocytes will themselves infiltrate and attack the thyroid gland.

SECONDARY ENDOCRINE HYPOFUNCTION

Secondary hypofunction is a distinct category of endocrine gland hypofunction in which the gland is basically intact but is dormant because it either is not stimulated or is directly inhibited. This form of hypofunction is reversible in that the gland begins working normally again if the stimulating hormone is supplied or if the inhibiting hormone or agent is removed. An example of secondary endocrine hypofunction is the loss of a stimulating (tropic) hormone that occurs as a result of pituitary gland destruction. In this situation, hormones are lost in a sequential order, beginning with growth hormone, followed by the gonadotropins, and followed by thyrotropin and adrenocorticotropin. Ultimately, there is growth failure and hypofunction of the gonads, thyroid gland, and adrenal glands.

OTHER CAUSES OF ENDOCRINE HYPOFUNCTION

Changes in biochemical environments may lead to endocrine hypofunction. A well-characterized example is the nutritional deficiency state caused by iodine deficiency. Iodine is an integral part of the thyroid hormone molecule, and it must be obtained from the diet. Hypothyroidism is common in areas of the world in which iodine levels in the soil are low and therefore the foods that are produced and consumed as the mainstay of the diet in those areas contain very small amounts of iodine. Drugs may also cause endocrine hypofunction. For example, patients with bipolar disorder are often treated with lithium, a drug that blocks thyroid hormone synthesis. Excess of one hormone that leads to the deficiency of another hormone can cause endocrine hypofunction. For example, overproduction of prolactin results in a secondary suppression of gonadal function, leading to amenorrhea (the abnormal cessation of menstruation) in women and impotence in men. These changes are reversed when the serum concentration of prolactin is reduced to normal.

Hormone deficiency can also occur as a result of defective hormonal action on target organs. This concept was first proposed in 1942 by American clinical endocrinologist Fuller Albright. Albright and his colleagues studied a young woman who had signs of parathormone deficiency but who, unlike other patients with parathormone deficiency, did not improve after the injection of an extract prepared from parathyroid glands. Albright described this disorder as pseudohypoparathyroidism and postulated that the disturbance is not a lack of parathormone but "an inability to respond to it." Direct evidence supporting this suggestion emerged decades later, and many other examples of unresponsiveness of target tissues to hormones have been documented since then. For example, an absence of androgen receptors causes people who are genetically male to appear to be female. In another example, some patients with diabetes mellitus do not respond to large quantities of insulin because they lack effective insulin receptors on target cells in the pancreas. In rare instances, a structurally abnormal hormone will not be recognized by its receptors on target cells, resulting in reduced biological activity of the hormone.

Endocrine hypofunction was once believed to be a cause of aging. However, the only well-documented endocrine hypofunction associated with age is the loss of ovarian hormones leading up to and during menopause. Even in postmenopausal women, however, the ovaries continue to produce small amounts of estrogens. In addition, there is a decline in the production of pituitary growth hormone and adrenal androgen with age in women and men and a decline in testicular function with age in men. For most other endocrine glands there may be no change or only a very small decrease in function. Whether the changes have survival value (or harm) is not clear.

ENDOCRINE HYPERFUNCTION

Endocrine glands that produce increased amounts of hormone are considered hyperfunctional and may undergo hypertrophy (increase in the size of each cell) and hyperplasia (increase in the number of cells). The hyperfunction may be primary, caused by some abnormality within the gland itself, or secondary (compensatory), caused by changes in the serum concentration of a substance that normally regulates the hormone and may in turn be regulated by the hormone. For example, patients diagnosed with primary hyperplasia of the parathyroid glands have increased serum calcium concentrations as a direct result of an abnormality of the parathyroid glands.

In contrast, patients diagnosed with secondary parathyroid hyperplasia have decreased serum calcium concentrations, resulting in stimulation of the parathyroid glands to produce more parathormone in an attempt to restore serum calcium concentrations to normal.

In certain instances, some of the cells of a gland affected by hyperplasia undergo a series of transformations that results in the formation of a tumour. In most cases, however, endocrine tumours arise from normal endocrine tissue. Endocrine tumours are largely autonomous, meaning that they are insensitive to any inhibition of hormone production imposed upon them through negative feedback control mechanisms.

Malignant tumours are not only hyperfunctional but are also capable of invading adjacent structures and spreading (metastasizing) to distant organs. While many endocrine tumours are hyperfunctional, others do not produce hormones at all.

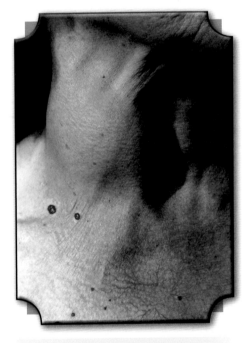

Excess hormone secretion and the resultant symptoms may be caused by intrinsic endocrine gland hyperplasia or tumours or by abnormal stimulation. Syndromes of endocrine hyperfunction may result when a small endocrine tumour, innocuous in itself, secretes excessive amounts of a stimulatory hormone, which then causes secondary hyperplasia of the target gland.

Elderly woman with a benign thyroid tumor. © www.istockphoto.com/Claudio Arnese

Some endocrine tumours produce excess quantities of the expected hormone and excess amounts of a hormone that is normally secreted by a different endocrine gland. In addition, tumours arising from tissues that ordinarily have no endocrine function may produce one or more hormones. A typical example is lung cancer, which may produce one or more of an array of hormones, most commonly vasopressin and adrenocorticotropin. Such tumours are called ectopic hormone-producing tumours.

ENDOCRINE-RELATED DEVELOPMENTAL DISORDERS

There are a number of growth and developmental disorders that arise from aberrant sexual differentiation during embryonic development. Many of these disorders result from abnormalities in the number of sex chromosomes. Humans possess a total of 46 chromosomes, two of which are sex chromosomes, designated X and Y. Individuals with two X chromosomes (XX) are female, and individuals with one X chromosome and one Y chromosome (XY) are male. Examples of conditions that affect sex chromosomes, and hence growth and development, include Klinefelter syndrome (47,XXY, 48,XXYY, 48,XXXY, 49,XXXYY, and 49,XXXXY), Turner syndrome (45,X, 46,XX, 45,X, and 47,XXX), and hermaphroditism (46,XX).

HERMAPHRODITISM

Hermaphroditism is the condition of having both male and female reproductive organs. Hermaphroditic plants (most flowering plants, or angiosperms) are called monoecious, or bisexual. Hermaphroditic animals—mostly invertebrates such as worms, bryozoans (moss animals), trematodes (flukes), snails, slugs, and barnacles—are usually parasitic, slow-moving, or permanently attached to another animal or plant.

In humans, hermaphroditism is an extremely rare sex anomaly. A true hermaphrodite is an individual who has both ovarian and testicular tissue. The ovarian and testicular tissue may be separate, or the two may be combined in what is called an ovotestis. Hermaphrodites have sex chromosomes showing male-female mosaicism (where one individual possesses both the male XY and female XX chromosome pairs). Most often, but not always, the chromosome complement is 46,XX, and in every such individual there also exists evidence of Y chromosomal material on one of the autosomes (any of the 22 pairs of chromosomes other than the sex chromosomes). Individuals with a 46,XX chromosome complement usually have ambiguous external genitalia with a sizable phallus and are therefore often reared as males. However, they develop breasts during puberty and menstruate and in only rare cases actually produce sperm. Individuals with the external appearance of one sex but the chromosomal constitution and reproductive organs of the opposite sex are examples of pseudohermaphroditism.

Treatment of hermaphroditism depends upon the age at which the diagnosis is made. If diagnosed at birth, choice of sex is usually made on the basis of the condition of the external genitalia (i.e., which sex organs predominate), after which surgery is performed to remove the gonads of the opposite sex. The remaining genitalia are then reconstructed to resemble those of the chosen sex. If it is decided that a male identity is deeply embedded and therefore a male role is preferable, all female tissues, including the oviducts and ovaries, are removed. In those persons to be reared as females, the male sexual tissues are removed. In older individuals the accepted gender is often

In July 2010, after nearly a year of uncertainty, the International Association of Athletics Federations (IAAF), the international body that governs track-and-field sports, cleared South African athlete Caster Semenya to compete as a woman. Semenya is seen here winning the world championship in the women's 800-m race in Berlin, Ger., Aug. 19, 2009. Semenya had come under medical scrutiny by the IAAF amid rumours she had an intersex condition that might impart a competitive advantage. Olivier Morin/AFP/Getty Images

reinforced by the appropriate surgical procedures and by hormonal therapy.

HYPOGONADISM

Hypogonadism is a disorder that affects males and is characterized by decreased testicular function resulting in testosterone deficiency and infertility. Hypogonadism is caused by hypothalamic, pituitary, and testicular diseases. Hypothalamic and pituitary diseases that may cause decreased testicular function include tumours and cysts of the hypothalamus, nonsecreting and prolactin-secreting pituitary tumours, trauma, hemochromatosis (excess iron storage), infections, and nonendocrine disorders, such as chronic illness and malnutrition. The primary testicular disorders that result in hypogonadism in postpubertal men include Klinefelter syndrome and related chromosomal disorders, although these disorders usually manifest at the time of puberty.

Other causes of hypogonadism in men include testicular inflammation (orchitis) caused by mumps; exposure to gonadal toxins, including alcohol, marijuana, and several anticancer drugs (e.g., cyclophosphamide, procarbazine, and platinum); and radiation with X-rays. Many of the disorders that cause delayed puberty are sufficiently mild that affected men do not seek care until well into adult life. This particularly applies to those disorders that decrease spermatogenesis and therefore fertility but spare Leydig cell function.

The clinical manifestations of hypogonadism in adult men include decreased libido, erectile dysfunction (inability to have or maintain an erection or to ejaculate), slowing of facial and pubic hair growth and thinning of hair in those regions, drying and thinning of the skin, weakness and loss of muscle mass, hot flashes, breast enlargement, infertility, small testes, and osteoporosis (bone thinning). The evaluation of men suspected to have hypogonadism should include measurements of serum testosterone, luteinizing hormone, follicle-stimulating hormone, and prolactin, in addition to the analysis of semen. Men with hypogonadism who have decreased or normal serum gonadotropin concentrations are said to have hypogonadotropic hypogonadism and may need to be evaluated for hypothalamic or pituitary disease with computerized axial tomography or magnetic resonance imaging (MRI) of the head. Men with hypogonadism who have increased serum gonadotropin concentrations are said to have hypergonadotropic hypogonadism, and their evaluation should be focused on the causes of testicular disease, including chromosomal disorders.

Men with hypogonadism caused by a hypothalamic disorder, pituitary disorder, or testicular disorder are treated with testosterone. Testosterone can be given by intramuscular injection or by patches or gels applied to the skin. Testosterone treatment reverses many of the symptoms and signs of hypogonadism but will not increase sperm count. Sperm count cannot be increased in men with testicular disease, although it is sometimes possible to increase sperm count in men with hypothalamic or pituitary disease by prolonged administration of gonadotropin-releasing hormone or gonadotropins. In men with testicular disease, viable sperm can sometimes be obtained by aspiration from the testes for in vitro fertilization.

KLINEFELTER SYNDROME

Klinefelter syndrome is a disorder of the human sex chromosomes that occurs in males. Klinefelter syndrome is one of the most frequent chromosomal disorders in males, occurring in approximately 1 in every 500 to 1,000 males. Men with Klinefelter syndrome have small, firm testes, and they often have breast enlargement (gynecomastia) and inordinately long legs and arms (eunuchoidism) and are infertile. Affected men have decreased serum testosterone concentrations, with urinary excretion of 17-ketosteroids (components of certain male hormones, or androgens) in the normal or low-normal range. They also have increased serum follicle-stimulating hormone and luteinizing hormone concentrations. Diabetes mellitus, goitre (enlargement of the thyroid gland), and various cancers may be more prevalent among Klinefelter syndrome patients. Thyroidal trapping of radioactive iodine and the responses of the thyroid to injections of thyrotropin may be low. Although normal in intelligence, some affected men have difficulties making social adjustments.

Klinefelter syndrome is named for Harry Klinefelter, an American physician who in 1942 described a set of symptoms that characterized the condition. The syndrome was first identified with a specific chromosomal abnormality in 1959 by British researcher Patricia A. Jacobs and her colleagues. It results from an unequal sharing of sex chromosomes very soon after fertilization, with one cell of a dividing pair receiving two X chromosomes and a Y chromosome and the other cell of the pair receiving only a Y chromosome and usually dying.

The normal male chromosome number and sex chromosome composition is 46,XY. However, because males with mosaic (tissues made up of genetically different cells) Klinefelter syndrome have an extra X chromosome, they typically have a chromosome composition of 47,XXY. Men with this form of the disorder usually have fewer symptoms than do men with the other chromosomal arrangements associated with Klinefelter syndrome. Other, rare chromosome complements that give rise to mosaic Klinefelter syndrome include 48,XXYY, 48,XXXY, 49,XXXYY, and 49,XXXXY. Men with these chromosome complements suffer from a variety of additional abnormalities, and, unlike men with 47,XXY Klinefelter syndrome, they often suffer from intellectual disability. One variant of the disorder in particular, the 49,XXXXY type, is characterized by fusion of the forearm bones and other skeletal anomalies, underdevelopment of the penis and scrotum, incomplete descent of the testes, and marked intellectual disability. Although about 40 percent of men affected by Klinefelter syndrome have a normal XY pattern, others possess a chromosome variant known as XX syndrome, in which Y chromosome material is transferred to an X chromosome or a nonsex chromosome (autosome). Men with XX syndrome have a male phenotype (physical appearance), but they have changes typical of Klinefelter syndrome.

Treatment with androgens reduces gynecomastia and evidence of male hypogonadism and increases strength and libido in patients with all variants of Klinefelter syndrome. In a few of these individuals, sperm obtained from the testes have successfully fertilized oocytes in vitro.

TURNER SYNDROME

Turner syndrome (or gonadal dysgenesis) is a relatively uncommon sex-chromosome disorder that causes aberrant sexual development in human females. Turner syndrome occurs when one sex chromosome is deleted, so that instead of the normal 46 chromosomes, of which two are sex chromosomes (XX in females and XY in males), the chromosomal complement is 45,X. In genetic terms, these patients are neither male nor female because the second, sex-determining chromosome is absent. However, phenotypically, affected individuals develop as females because there is no Y chromosome to direct the fetal gonads to the male configuration.

Clinically, patients with Turner syndrome are short, and they have a small chin, prominent folds of skin at the inner corners of the eyes (epicanthal folds), low-set ears, a webbed neck, and a shieldlike chest. Individuals with Turner syndrome also have an increased incidence of anomalies of the heart and large blood vessels. Both the internal and the external genitalia are infantile, and the ovaries are only "streaks" of connective tissue. The diagnosis may be made during infancy or childhood on the basis of these anomalies or at puberty when the individual fails to develop second-ary sex characteristics or has no menses. In genetic terms, Turner syndrome is common: one-tenth of all spontane-ously aborted fetuses have a 45,X chromosome constitution, and only 3 percent of affected fetuses survive to term.

Patients with Turner syndrome can be treated with growth hormone during childhood to increase linear growth. Affected individuals should also be treated with estrogen and progestin (similar to proges-terone) at the time of puberty in order to stimulate the appearance of secondary sexual characteristics and the monthly vaginal bleeding that simulates a menstrual cycle. Estrogen and progestin also prevent osteoporo-sis, which will occur if ovarian deficiency is not treated.

There are multiple variants of Turner syndrome. For example, there are mixtures of chromosomes (mosaics), such as a 45,X and 46,XX chromosomal complement or a 45,X and 47,XXX chromosomal complement, and chro-mosomal translocations, in which a portion of one chromosome is transferred to another chromosome. Another variant is the 45,X/46,XY mosaic, in which a per-son may be reared as either a male or a female because the genitalia are "ambiguous," meaning that it is difficult to determine whether the phallus is an enlarged clitoris or a small penis. Patients with this variant of Turner syndrome have streak gonads, and the presence of the Y chromo-some is associated with an increased risk of development of a malignant tumour of the streak gonad.

ECTOPIC HORMONE AND POLYGLANDULAR DISORDERS

There are several syndromes of hormone hypersecretion that are caused by the unregulated production of hormones, usually by tumours. Ectopic hormone production involves the synthesis and secretion of peptide or protein hormones by benign or malignant tumours of tissues that do not normally synthesize and secrete the particular hormone. The hormone that is most commonly produced ectopically is adrenocorticotropic hormone (ACTH). This syndrome occurs most often in patients with small-cell carcinomas of the lung (SCLC), but it can occur in patients with carcinoid tumours (benign or malignant tumours that secrete hormonelike substances such as serotonin), islet-cell tumours of the pancreas, and carcinomas of many other organs. Many patients with ectopic corticotropin production have intense pigmentation, caused by hypersecretion of adrenocorticotropin, and severe depletion of potassium (hypokalemia), caused by high serum cortisol concentrations. Treatment ordinarily involves surgical removal or drug-induced destruction of the tumour. However, in cases in which the tumour cannot be removed or its function reduced, adrenalectomy (removal of the adrenal glands) or treatment with a drug such as ketoconazole, an antifungal drug that inhibits adrenal steroid synthesis, may be more effective.

Ectopic hormone production can result in numerous abnormal hormone-related physiological conditions, including hypercalcemia (increased serum calcium concentrations), hyponatremia (decreased serum sodium concentrations), hypoglycemia (decreased blood sugar concentrations), and acromegaly (excess production of growth hormone). Tumour-induced hormone production (or production of hormonelike substances) can cause many of these conditions. For example, hypercalcemia can be caused by tumour production of parathyroid-hormone-related protein (structurally similar to parathormone) or, rarely, by tumour production of parathormone, 1,25-dihydroxyvitamin D_3 (the active form of vitamin D in animal tissues; sometimes called calcitriol, or 1,25-dihydroxycholecalciferol), or interleukins (mediators of immune response). Hypercalcemia can also be caused by the invasion and destruction of bone tissue by a tumour. Hyponatremia can occur as a result of vasopressin secretion, usually by small-cell carcinomas of the lung, and hypoglycemia may be caused by tumour production of insulin-like growth factors or, very rarely, insulin. Treatment is aimed at removing the offending tumour, reducing the size or activity of the tumour, or mitigating the effects of the hormone that is produced in excess.

Production of thyrotropin, luteinizing hormone, and follicle-stimulating hormone by nonpituitary tumours does not occur. Similarly, the production of steroid or thyroid hormones by tumours of tissues that do not normally produce these hormones does not occur. This may be because these hormones have a high degree of structural complexity, with multiple rings, chains of amino acids, and carbohydrate molecules, and the production of these hormones is dependent upon genes expressed by the tumour that are required to produce the multiple enzymes involved in hormone synthesis. Human chorionic gonadotropin, which is structurally similar to luteinizing hormone and has similar biological properties, is produced by tumours of cells of embryonic origin, such as hepatoblastomas and chorionic tumours (e.g., hydatidiform moles and choriocarcinomas), and is occasionally produced by other tumours. The clinical effects of excess chorionic gonadotropin production include precocious pubertal development in children, ovarian hyperstimulation in women, and estrogen excess in men. Chorionic tumours that produce very large amounts of chorionic gonadotropin can cause hyperthyroidism, since this hormone also has weak thyroid-stimulating activity.

There also are several genetic disorders characterized by hormone-producing tumours of several endocrine glands. In these disorders, known as multiple endocrine neoplasia (MEN), affected patients have germ line mutations (heritable mutations that are incorporated into all of the cells of the body) in genes that predispose them to endocrine gland hyperplasia and tumour development. The tumours may occur in more than one endocrine gland and may appear simultaneously or at varying times in the course of the disease. The embryonic origin of the cells of the endocrine glands that are involved may also be different. In addition, there exist multiple endocrine deficiency disorders (polyglandular autoimmune syndrome), in which affected persons have deficiencies of multiple endocrine glands caused by autoimmune destruction of the glands. Multiple endocrine deficiency disorders result in multiple hormonal deficiencies and are suspected to be caused by underlying heritable genetic mutations.

MULTIPLE ENDOCRINE NEOPLASIA

Multiple endocrine neoplasia (MEN) is any of a group of rare hereditary disorders in which tumours occur in multiple glands of the endocrine system. The disorders are transmitted in an autosomal dominant fashion, meaning that defects can occur in males and females, and, statistically, half the children of an affected person will also be affected. Multiple endocrine neoplasia is often difficult to recognize in its early stages because the pattern of endocrine gland hyperplasia and tumour development varies. In addition, the tumours that characterize the syndromes of multiple endocrine neoplasia do not appear simultaneously. Thus, a patient may have incomplete expression of one of these inherited syndromes when first examined. However, many of these individuals will later develop other tumours or conditions that are characteristic of a particular type of multiple endocrine neoplasia.

MEN1

The first described and the most frequently occurring of these rare disorders is multiple endocrine neoplasia 1 (MEN1). The principal glands involved in this syndrome are the parathyroid glands, the pancreatic islets of Langerhans, and the anterior pituitary gland. Patients with tumours of two of these three glands are considered to have MEN1. If one family member has been diagnosed with the disorder and a first-degree relative has a tumour of one of the three glands, the condition is defined as familial MEN1. The most common disorder associated with MEN1 is primary hyperparathyroidism (characterized by the presence of parathyroid adenomas—noncancerous tumours that develop from glandular cells—or hyperplasia), which occurs in about 90 percent of patients. Coinciding disorders may include pancreatic islet-cell tumours, such as gastric acid-secreting tumours (gastrinomas), pancreatic polypeptide-secreting tumours, insulin-secreting tumours (insulinomas), and, less commonly, glucagon-secreting, vasoactive intestinal polypeptide-secreting, or somatostatin-secreting tumours.

About 20 percent of cases present as nonsecreting pituitary adenomas or as pituitary adenomas that secrete prolactin or growth hormone. Carcinoid (serotonin-secreting) tumours and tumours of the adrenal cortex may occur, but they may be coincidental rather than an integral part of the disorder.

Treatment usually consists of surgery for patients with hyperparathyroidism, insulinomas, or growth hormone-secreting and nonsecreting pituitary tumours. Because dopamine is an effective prolactin-inhibiting factor, a dopamine agonist (a drug that increases dopamine activity) may be used for patients with prolactin-secreting pituitary tumours. Surgery or a proton pump inhibitor (a drug that blocks gastric acid secretion) may be used for patients with gastrinomas to decrease levels of gastric acid and the occurrence of peptic ulcers.

Most patients with MEN1, as well as people with a familial risk of developing MEN1, have germ line mutations (mutations that affect all cells in the body) in a tumour suppressor gene designated *MEN1*. This gene codes for a protein called menin that normally helps prevent neoplastic proliferation (uncontrolled new growth) of cells. Mutations in *MEN1* lead to the synthesis of a form of menin that is less active in preventing neoplastic proliferation. The *MEN1* gene is expressed in many tissues, including nonendocrine tissues, and it is not understood why mutations in *MEN1* result in tumours only in endocrine glands.

Mutation testing in affected patients confirms diagnosis of MEN1, and testing in asymptomatic family members identifies whether they are at risk of developing MEN1. People who carry mutations in *MEN1* should be evaluated periodically by history and physical examination and measurements of serum concentrations of calcium, gastrin, and prolactin. Detecting the development of MEN1 in its early stages is important because early treatment is more effective and safer than treatment of more advanced disease.

MEN2

Multiple endocrine neoplasia 2 (MEN2) is characterized by a different constellation of endocrine abnormalities than MEN1. Conditions associated with MEN2 include medullary carcinoma of the thyroid gland, pheochromocytomas (tumours characterized by high blood pressure), hyperparathyroidism, ganglioneuromas (tumours derived from cells originating in the neural crest during embryological development), and a tall, lean body with long extremities. If one family member has been diagnosed with medullary thyroid carcinoma and a first-degree relative is diagnosed with any manifestation of the disorder, the condition is defined as familial MEN2. There are three forms of the disorder: MEN2A (accounting for about 75 percent of affected families), familial medullary thyroid carcinoma (FMTC-only; accounting for 5 to 20 percent of affected families), and MEN2B (accounting for less than 5 percent of affected families).

The primary tumour type found in patients with MEN2A is medullary thyroid carcinoma, which occurs in at least 90 percent of affected patients. This is followed by pheochromocytoma, often bilateral (meaning that it occurs in both adrenal glands), in about 50 percent of patients and primary hyperparathyroidism in about 20 percent of patients. The least common form of MEN2, MEN2B, is characterized by medullary thyroid carcinoma in 95 percent of patients, bilateral pheochromocytoma in about 50 percent of patients, intestinal or mucosal ganglioneuromas (benign tumours of the lips, tongue, and lining of the mouth, throat, and intestine) in about 95 percent of patients (but not primary hyperparathyroidism), and a tall, lean physical appearance in roughly 50 percent of patients. Patients and families with FMTC-only should be studied very carefully to be sure affected family members do not have other features of MEN2A or MEN2B.

Medullary thyroid carcinoma arises from the parafollicular, or C cells, of the thyroid gland, and is nearly always the first manifestation of MEN2. It can occur in very young children and is preceded by hyperplasia of the C cells. Patients with pheochromocytomas should be treated surgically as well. Unlike MEN1, in which several drugs are available to control hormone overproduction by some glands, there is no effective treatment for the other components of MEN2.

Nearly all patients with MEN2 and FMTC-only have germ line mutations in the *RET* (rearranged during transfection) proto-oncogene (a gene susceptible to mutations that transform it into an oncogene, or cancer-inducing gene). The *RET* gene codes for a transmembrane protein receptor that contains an intracellular signaling region called a tyrosine kinase domain. The kinase domain is fundamental in activating cell signaling cascades. Kinase activity causes the transfer of high-energy phosphate molecules to tyrosine residues on nearby proteins, resulting in protein activation and initiation of downstream signaling events. These signaling events culminate in specific cellular functions, such as promoting cell survival and differentiation. Mutations in *RET* that are associated with MEN2 cause the kinase domain to be constantly active (gain-of-function mutations), which predisposes the cells to tumour formation because cell death signaling pathways are inhibited and proliferation pathways are stimulated. The *RET* gene is expressed in multiple types of tissues, including nonendocrine tissues, and it is not clear why the mutations in this gene that are associated with MEN2 primarily affect only the C cells of the thyroid and the cells of the adrenal medulla.

Because medullary thyroid carcinoma occurs in nearly all individuals who carry a mutation in *RET* and because it appears at an early age, it is important that all patients with medullary thyroid carcinoma be tested for mutations in *RET*. If a mutation is found, all family members should be tested for that specific mutation, and prophylactic total thyroidectomy should be done in those who carry the mutation. The timing of the operation depends on the mutation. Patients carrying some mutations should undergo thyroidectomy within the first year of life, before medullary thyroid carcinoma has appeared. In other patients, operations can be delayed until adolescence. Given the lower likelihood of pheochromocytoma and hyperparathyroidism, prophylactic adrenalectomy or parathyroidectomy is not recommended. Family members who do not have the mutation do not need to undergo screening for tumours or prophylactic surgery.

PHEOCHROMOCYTOMA

Pheochromocytoma (or chromaffinoma) is a tumour, most often nonmalignant, that causes abnormally high blood pressure (hypertension) because of hypersecretion of the hormones epinephrine and norepinephrine. Usually the tumour is in the medullary cells of the adrenal gland. However, it may arise from extra-adrenal chromaffin tissue, which may be located in the sympathetic nervous system adjacent to the vertebral column anywhere from the neck to the pelvis or even in the urinary bladder.

Pheochromocytomas can cause striking symptoms and signs. Hypertension is an invariable finding in patients with these tumours. It may be constant, mimicking the common forms of hypertension, or episodic and associated with headache, excessive perspiration, heart palpitation, pallor, tremour, and anxiety. Episodic attacks may end abruptly, and the patient may appear normal afterward. The attacks may last a few minutes to several hours, and they may occur at intervals that range from once a month to several per day. Most pheochromocytomas secrete norepinephrine. In persons with tumours that secrete an appreciable amount of epinephrine, anxiety may be increased, and the patient may experience weight loss and fever and have diabetes mellitus.

Most pheochromocytomas are sporadic, but they also occur in patients with several hereditary tumour syndromes, including MEN2 and von Hippel–Lindau syndrome. The presence of a pheochromocytoma can be confirmed by measurements of epinephrine and norepinephrine or by measurements of degradation products of these substances in serum or urine. The tumour itself can also be identified by imaging procedures.

Patients with a pheochromocytoma are treated surgically and should receive preoperative treatment with both an alpha-adrenergic drug and a beta-adrenergic antagonist drug to ameliorate hypertension and prevent marked fluctuations of epinephrine and norepinephrine during the operation. Patients with a malignant pheochromocytoma are treated with antagonist drugs indefinitely.

POLYGLANDULAR AUTOIMMUNE SYNDROME

Polyglandular autoimmune syndrome is either of two familial syndromes in which affected patients have multiple endocrine gland deficiencies. Some patients produce serum antibodies that react with, and presumably damage, multiple endocrine glands and other tissues, and other patients produce lymphocytes (a type of white blood cell) that migrate into and damage endocrine glands.

Type 1 polyglandular autoimmune syndrome occurs in children or adolescents and is characterized primarily by hypoparathyroidism (deficiency of parathormone), infection with the fungal organism *Candida albicans*, which causes candidiasis of the skin or the mucous membrane of the mouth, and adrenal insufficiency (Addison disease). Affected patients may also have diabetes mellitus, hypogonadism (inadequate secretion of sex hormones and development of sex organs), hypothyroidism (decreased secretion of thyroid hormone), or intestinal malabsorption. Type 1 polyglandular autoimmune syndrome is inherited as an autosomal recessive trait (the abnormal gene must be inherited from both parents) and is caused by a mutation in the *AIRE* (autoimmune regulator) gene.

Type 2 polyglandular autoimmune syndrome occurs in adults and is characterized by adrenal insufficiency, type I diabetes mellitus, hypothyroidism or Graves disease, hypogonadism, and pernicious anemia. Type 2 polyglandular autoimmune syndrome may affect multiple members of a family, but the pattern of inheritance is not known.

ENDOCRINE CHANGES WITH AGING

Because the endocrine glands play pivotal roles both in reproduction and in development, it seems plausible to extend the role of the endocrine system to account for the progressive changes in body structure and function that occur with aging (senescence). Indeed, years ago an "endocrine theory of aging" enjoyed wide popularity, but it is now clear that—with some exceptions—endocrine function does not significantly change with age.

The greatest change is in ovarian function, which decreases abruptly following menopause. There are gradual age-related decreases in the production of melatonin, growth hormone and insulin-like growth factor 1 (IGF-1), and dehydroepiandrosterone (DHEA). The recognition of these decreases has led to the view that administration of these hormones might somehow slow the process of aging. However, there is no scientific evidence that administration of these or any other hormones mitigates, much less reverses, any of the biological changes of aging.

As longevity in the United States increases, so too does the definition of "senior citizen." Witness Jane Bulger, who attended the original 1969 Woodstock concert, displaying said redefinition by exuberantly celebrating the 40-year anniversary of the famed event in Bethel, N.Y. Mario Tama/Getty Images

MENOPAUSE

The most striking age-related change in endocrine function is menopause. Estrogens are produced by granulosa and interstitial cells, which line the egg-containing ovarian follicles. The depletion of ovarian follicles with age makes a reduction in estrogen secretion inevitable, and this decrease defines the onset of menopause. In postmenopausal women, serum estrogen concentrations decrease by at least 80 percent. This decrease leads to increases in the secretion and serum concentrations of follicle-stimulating hormone and luteinizing hormone. Increases in the secretion and serum concentrations of these hormones provide evidence that the pituitary gland remains functional in normal postmenopausal women, even though ovarian function declines markedly.

TESTICULAR CHANGES

Serum testosterone concentrations decrease very gradually in men beginning around age 30. Men aged 70 or older may have substantially reduced testosterone levels. About 2 percent of men are affected by late-onset hypogonadism (andropause, or male menopause), which begins around age 40 and results in decreased testicular function and testosterone deficiency. Symptoms of late-onset hypogonadism include decreased libido, fatigue, depression, and erectile dysfunction. The condition may proceed unnoticed for many years because symptoms are often subtle.

The normal physiological decline of testosterone in men is due to a decrease in the number of androgen-secreting Leydig cells and is accompanied by a gradual decrease in spermatogenesis, although men often remain fertile for many more years. In addition, there is a small compensatory increase in gonadotropin secretion.

CHANGES IN THYROID AND ADRENAL FUNCTION

Thyroid function does not significantly change with age. The clearance of thyroxine and triiodothyronine decreases somewhat and is matched by a decrease in their production. Therefore, serum thyroxine and triiodothyronine concentrations do not change, nor do serum thyrotropin concentrations. As many as 10 to 12 percent of people age 60 years and older have slightly increased serum thyrotropin concentrations because of mild chronic autoimmune thyroiditis. Similarly, adrenocorticotropin and cortisol secretion do not significantly change with age, but serum DHEA concentrations decrease progressively beginning at about 30 years of age. The cause of the decrease in dehydroepiandrosterone is not known. The secretion of aldosterone also decreases slightly, as does plasma renin activity, but healthy elderly people are able to maintain normal fluid and electrolyte balance.

FLUCTUATIONS IN GROWTH HORMONE SECRETION

Growth hormone secretion and serum IGF-1 concentrations decrease gradually with age. As compared with young adults, older people have mild deficiency of growth hormone and IGF-1. Deficiency of IGF-1 could help to explain the decrease of muscle mass and the increase in fat mass that occurs in many older people. Whether growth hormone treatment reverses these changes is controversial, and the treatment has potentially dangerous side effects, including increased blood pressure and fluid retention.

CHANGES IN PARATHORMONE SECRETION AND BONE

Parathormone secretion tends to increase slightly with age, but serum calcium concentrations do not significantly change. The possible reasons for increased secretion of parathormone include decreased calcium and vitamin D intake (and possibly decreased sun exposure) and decreased kidney function that causes a reduction in the amount of vitamin D that an older individual can absorb.

Peak bone mass and density occur at about age 30. Thereafter bone mass declines gradually with age. The decline accelerates during the first years after menopause in women, after which the rate of loss slows but nonetheless continues indefinitely. This loss of bone contributes to the well-known increase in fractures that occur in elderly people, especially in women. A very important contributing factor to an increased risk of fracture is an increased likelihood of falls, caused by decreases in muscle strength and coordination. The risk factors for loss of bone in older people include genetic susceptibility, smoking, lean body build, inactivity, calcium and vitamin D deficiency, and estrogen deficiency in women and testosterone deficiency in men.

CHANGES IN VASOPRESSIN CONCENTRATIONS

Older people tend to have decreased thirst in response to water deprivation and increased basal serum vasopressin concentrations. In addition, their kidneys tend to respond less well to vasopressin when compared with younger people. These changes increase the risk of dehydration. On the other hand, if water is available, increased vasopressin secretion may result in an increase in water retention and decreased serum sodium concentrations (hyponatremia).

FLUCTUATIONS IN GLUCOSE AND INSULIN METABOLISM

Blood glucose concentrations, while usually normal in the fasting state, increase after the ingestion of glucose in increments proportional to the age of the subject. That is, the older the subject, the higher the increase in blood glucose after glucose ingestion. The accompanying increase in insulin secretion, although appreciable, is not sufficient to maintain blood glucose concentrations in the range found in healthy young adults. Whether these changes should be viewed as abnormal or whether they merely reflect modifications appropriate to the aging process remains a matter of debate.

CHAPTER 5

DISEASES AND DISORDERS OF THE THYROID AND PARATHYROID GLANDS

Diseases and disorders of the thyroid and parathyroid glands are distinguished by their effects on metabolism. In the case of the thyroid, disease leads to altered metabolism and growth (in children) and typically causes either increased or decreased function of multiple organ systems. In contrast, dysfunction of the parathyroids generally is limited to changes in the metabolism of calcium and phosphate, with consequent effects on bone.

DISEASES AND DISORDERS OF THE THYROID GLAND

The most recognizable symptom of disease of the thyroid is goitre, which is the name given to any enlargement of the gland. The most common thyroid disease is thyroid nodular disease (the appearance of small, usually benign lumps within an otherwise healthy gland), followed by hypothyroidism (reduced secretion of thyroid hormone), hyperthyroidism (excess secretion of thyroid hormone), and thyroid cancer.

GOITRE

Goitre is an enlargement of the thyroid gland that produces a prominent swelling in the front of the neck. The normal human thyroid gland weighs 10 to 20 grams (about

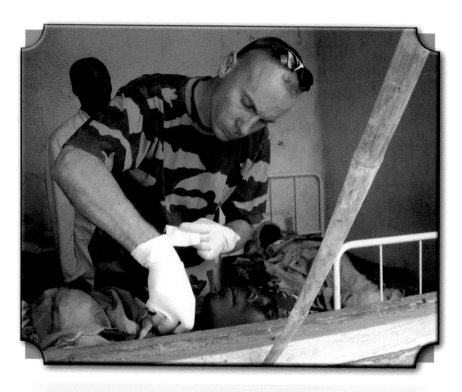

Andjouma Ramadan, a goitre patient in Chad, is examined Feb. 11, 2009, by French Corp. Laurent Beaupeliet, a member of the French military medical staff then serving on a European Union mission to help restore stability to the conflict-torn central-African state. Georges Gobet/AFP/Getty Images

0.3 to 0.6 ounce), and some goitrous thyroid glands weigh as much as 1,000 grams (more than 2 pounds). The entire thyroid gland may be enlarged, or there may be one or more large thyroid nodules. The function of the thyroid gland may be decreased, normal, or increased. A very large goitre may cause sensations of choking and can cause difficulty in breathing and swallowing.

The most common type of goitre is endemic goitre, caused by iodine deficiency. Iodine is an essential nutrient that is required for the production of thyroid hormone. When iodine intake is low, thyroid hormone production is low, and in response the pituitary gland secretes greater quantities of the hormone thyrotropin in an attempt to restore thyroid hormone production to normal. This excess thyrotropin stimulates not only thyroid hormone production but also thyroid growth. Endemic goitre is more common among girls than boys and among women than men. It occurs most frequently in inland or mountainous regions where the natural iodine content of the water and soil is very low. It can be easily prevented by use of salt or food to which iodine has been added. In young people, increasing iodine intake results in regression of the goitre. However, the likelihood of regression diminishes with age. Surgical removal of the thyroid gland may be necessary if the goitre causes breathing or swallowing problems.

There are numerous other causes and types of goitre. One is caused by a defect in one of the steps in the synthesis of thyroid hormone. Like iodine deficiency, these defects result in increased thyrotropin secretion. More-common causes are one or multiple nodules in the thyroid (uninodular or multinodular goitre), infiltration of the thyroid by lymphocytes or other inflammatory cells (thyroiditis), or stimulation of thyroid growth (and function) by antibodies that activate the thyroid in the same way as does thyrotropin, as occurs in the disorder called Graves disease.

GRANULOMATOUS THYROIDITIS

Granulomatous thyroiditis (also called subacute thyroiditis, giant-cell thyroiditis, pseudotuberculous thyroiditis, or de Quervain thyroiditis) is an inflammatory disease of the thyroid gland of unknown but presumably viral origin. It may persist from several weeks to a few months but subsides spontaneously.

The disease most frequently occurs in women. The thyroid gland becomes enlarged, and most patients complain of tenderness in the front of the throat and difficulty in swallowing. Other symptoms include those of hyperthyroidism (e.g., accelerated heart rate, sweating, tremor), which are transient, and thyroid gland pain, fatigue, muscle aches, and fever. Most patients with the disease require only mild pain relievers for alleviation of symptoms, although more severe cases may call for stronger drugs, including glucocorticoids.

GRAVES DISEASE

Graves disease (also called toxic diffuse goitre, or exophthalmic goitre) is the most common cause of hyperthyroidism and thyrotoxicosis (effects of excess thyroid hormone action in tissue). In Graves disease the excessive secretion of thyroid hormone is accompanied by diffuse enlargement of the thyroid gland (diffuse goitre). The thyroid gland may be slightly enlarged or several times its normal size. The increased thyroid hormone production results in the symptoms and signs of hyperthyroidism. Some patients also experience exophthalmos (protrusion of the eyes), with eyelid retraction, edema of tissues surrounding the eyes, double vision, and occasionally loss of vision, all of which are symptoms of a condition known as Graves ophthalmopathy.

Graves disease is an autoimmune disease (i.e., when the body reacts to its own tissues as though they were foreign substances). Patients with Graves disease produce antibodies that act on the thyroid to increase thyroid hormone production and thyroid size. These same, or closely related, antibodies may cause Graves ophthalmopathy. Graves disease occurs in women four to six times as often as in men. It most often affects young to middle-aged adults but can occur at all ages. The underlying cause of Graves disease is not known, but there is genetic susceptibility to the disease, and smoking is a risk factor, especially for Graves ophthalmopathy. Another characteristic of the disease is spontaneous remission of hyperthyroidism, which occurs in 30 to 40 percent of patients.

There is no treatment for Graves disease itself. Hyperthyroidism is treated with an antithyroid drug, radioactive iodine, or, rarely, surgical removal of the thyroid.

Graves ophthalmopathy occurs in approximately 25 percent of patients with Graves disease. It usually occurs as the patient is developing hyperthyroidism, but it can occur after hyperthyroidism is treated. There is no simple, effective treatment for the eye disease, and it may persist for years. Patients with severe inflammation of the tissues that surround the eye or with impairment of vision may be treated with a glucocorticoid or surgical decompression of the orbits.

Approximately 2 percent of patients with Graves disease have what is called localized myxedema. This is characterized by painless lumps composed of edematous subcutaneous tissue and thickening of the overlying skin on the lower legs (sometimes called pretibial myxedema) or, rarely, the arms or trunk. Nearly all patients with localized myxedema have had hyperthyroidism in the past and have severe ophthalmopathy. The only effective treatment is application of a glucocorticoid to the affected areas of skin.

Irish physician Robert Graves (1796 –1853), for whom Graves disease is named, was among the first to describe the condition. SPL/Photo Researchers, Inc.

HASHIMOTO DISEASE

Hashimoto disease (also called Hashimoto thyroiditis, chronic lymphocytic thyroiditis, chronic autoimmune thyroiditis, or struma lymphomatosa) is another autoimmune disorder. It is characterized by a gradual enlargement of the thyroid gland and a gradual decrease in thyroid hormone production. The usual findings are symmetrical rubbery enlargement of the thyroid gland, symptoms and signs of hypothyroidism, or both. The natural course of the disease often includes gradually increasing thyroid enlargement, as well as increasing thyroid deficiency. However, spontaneous improvement in hypothyroidism or goitre can occur. Pathologic examination of the thyroid reveals infiltration by white blood cells called lymphocytes and excess growth (hyperplasia) of thyroid tissue. The majority of patients are women, who are five to eight times more likely to develop this condition than men. It occurs more frequently in older women. There is a genetic predisposition to the disease, and a high iodine intake may contribute to its onset.

Patients with Hashimoto thyroiditis have antibodies against several components of thyroid tissue in their serum. Among them are antibodies against the enzyme thyroid peroxidase and the thyroid protein thyroglobulin. These antibodies are often measured as a diagnostic test for the disease, but they do not alter thyroid function or damage the thyroid. Some patients with the disease produce antibodies that block the action of thyrotropin. In most patients the thyroid is gradually destroyed, either by antibodies that damage the thyroid cells (cytotoxic antibodies) or, more likely, by lymphocytes that have been sensitized to migrate to the thyroid, where they interact with thyroid cells and produce substances (cytokines) that damage thyroid cells. The factors that initiate this process or the particular substances that cause the thyroid damage are not known.

There is no treatment for Hashimoto disease itself. Hypothyroidism is treated with thyroid hormone, usually thyroxine, which may also reduce the size of a goitre, if present.

HYPERCALCITONINEMIA

Hypercalcitoninemia is characterized by an abnormally high blood concentration of calcitonin. In humans and other mammals, the condition is often indicative of a nutritional disorder or a thyroid disorder. In humans, hypercalcitoninemia is most frequently associated with medullary thyroid carcinomas. Hypercalcitoninemia may also occur as a side effect of certain drugs, including beta-blockers, which are agents commonly used in the treatment of heart failure, and omeprazole, which is a proton-pump inhibitor used in the treatment of peptic ulcer.

HYPERTHYROIDISM

Hyperthyroidism (or thyrotoxicosis) is the excess production of thyroid hormone by the thyroid gland. Most patients with hyperthyroidism have an enlarged thyroid gland (goitre), but the characteristics of the enlargement vary. Hyperthyroidism occurs more often in adults than in children, and it is 5 to 10 times more common in women than in men.

The most common cause of hyperthyroidism is Graves disease, named for the Irish physician Robert Graves, who was among the first to describe the condition. The second most common cause of hyperthyroidism is toxic multinodular goitre, or Plummer disease. A less common cause of hyperthyroidism is a benign tumour (toxic adenoma) of the thyroid gland. In many cases these tumours contain a mutation of the thyrotropin receptor gene that results in the synthesis of thyrotropin receptors that are active and therefore lead to excess thyroid hormone production in the absence of thyrotropin.

Several types of thyroiditis can result in the release of stored thyroid hormone in amounts sufficient to cause hyperthyroidism. One type, called silent lymphocytic thyroiditis, is painless and is particularly common in women in the first year after a pregnancy (postpartum thyroiditis). Another type, called subacute granulomatous thyroiditis, is characterized by thyroid pain and tenderness. Hyperthyroidism in patients with thyroiditis is usually mild and self-limiting, lasting only until the stores of hormone in the thyroid gland are exhausted.

The administration of high doses of thyroid hormone is a common cause of hyperthyroidism. The hormone may have been given by a physician to treat hypothyroidism or to decrease the size of a goitre. In addition, some patients purchase thyroid hormone from health and nutrition stores in the form of a crude thyroid extract or an analogue of thyroid hormone purported to stimulate metabolism and cause weight loss. These preparations may contain variable amounts of thyroid hormone and can have unpredictable effects on the body. In rare cases, hyperthyroidism may be caused by a thyrotropin-secreting tumour of the pituitary gland or a struma ovarii, in which hyperfunctioning thyroid tissue is present in a tumour of the ovary.

The onset of hyperthyroidism is usually gradual but can be sudden. The increase in thyroid hormone secretion results in an increase in the function of many organ systems. The cardiovascular and neuromuscular systems are likely to be affected. The cardiovascular symptoms and signs of hyperthyroidism include an increase in heart rate (tachycardia), atrial fibrillation (rapid irregular heart rhythm), palpitations (pounding in the chest due to forceful contraction of the heart), shortness of breath, and exercise intolerance. Neuromuscular symptoms and signs of hyperthyroidism include nervousness, hyperactivity and restlessness, anxiety and irritability, insomnia, tremor, and muscle weakness. Other common symptoms and signs of hyperthyroidism are weight loss despite a good or even increased appetite, increased perspiration and intolerance of heat, increased frequency of bowel movements, and irregular menstrual cycles and decreased menstrual blood flow in women. Hyperthyroidism also causes an increase in bone resorption and therefore contributes to osteoporosis. The most severe form of hyperthyroidism is thyroid storm. This acute condition is characterized by very rapid heart rate, fever, and severe symptoms and may result in heart failure, low blood pressure (hypotension), and death.

Hyperthyroidism is diagnosed based on the symptoms and signs described above and on measurements of high serum total and free thyroid hormone concentrations and low, sometimes undetectable, serum thyrotropin concentrations. In serum, thyroid hormones exist in two forms, one of which is bound to several proteins, and the other of which, a very small amount, is free. Thus, serum thyroxine can be measured as serum total thyroxine or free thyroxine. The latter is preferable because it is the form of thyroxine that is readily available to the cells of the body and, therefore, is metabolically active. Measurements of serum total thyroxine are high in patients with thyroid disease and in patients producing more of the proteins that bind to thyroxine.

The cause of hyperthyroidism may be distinguished based on relative differences in the concentrations of thyroxine, triiodothyronine, and thyrotropin. Patients with a thyrotropin-secreting pituitary tumour have normal or high serum thyrotropin concentrations. Rarely, patients have normal serum thyroxine concentrations but high serum triiodothyronine concentrations. These patients are said to have triiodothyronine thyrotoxicosis. Other patients have low serum thyrotropin concentrations but normal serum thyroxine and triiodothyronine concentrations, with few or no symptoms and signs of hyperthyroidism. These patients are said to have subclinical hyperthyroidism. Thyroid uptake of radioiodine may be measured to distinguish thyroiditis or excess thyroid hormone administration, in which the thyroid uptake is low, from other causes of hyperthyroidism, in which the thyroid uptake is high.

Hyperthyroidism is usually a chronic, even lifelong, disorder. It can be treated with an antithyroid drug, radioactive iodine, or surgery (thyroidectomy), in which a portion or all of the thyroid gland is surgically removed. There are three widely used antithyroid drugs—methimazole, carbimazole (which is rapidly converted to methimazole in the body), and propylthiouracil. These drugs block the production of thyroid hormone but have no permanent effect on either the thyroid gland or the underlying cause of the hyperthyroidism. Patients with hyperthyroidism caused by Graves disease are often treated with an antithyroid drug for one to two years in the hope that they will have a remission of the disease and remain well after the drug is stopped. This is successful in 30 to 50 percent of patients. Radioactive iodine is taken up by thyroid cells in the same way as is nonradioactive iodine, but the radiation destroys the cells, thereby reducing thyroid hormone production and also reducing the size of the thyroid gland. It is highly effective, but it results ultimately in hypothyroidism in most patients. It is suitable for patients with Graves disease and is the preferred treatment for patients with a nodular goitre, in whom hyperthyroidism is a lifelong condition. The removal of the thyroid by thyroidectomy is rarely performed, except in the case of patients with a large goitre. When caused by thyroiditis, hyperthyroidism is transient, usually lasting only four to six weeks or at most two months. Most patients need no treatment or only symptomatic treatment with a beta-adrenergic antagonist drug (beta-blocker).

HYPOTHYROIDISM

Hypothyroidism is a deficiency in hormone production by the thyroid gland. Hypothyroidism usually results from a disorder of the thyroid gland, in which case it is described as primary hypothyroidism. Congenital primary hypothyroidism is caused by lack of or abnormal development of the thyroid in utero and inherited defects in the synthesis of thyroid hormone. A major cause of acquired primary hypothyroidism is chronic autoimmune thyroiditis. This condition has two forms: the earlier-described Hashimoto disease, characterized by goitre, and atrophic thyroiditis, which is characterized by the shrinkage of the thyroid gland. There also exists a form of hypothyroidism known as central hypothyroidism, in which there is a deficiency of thyrotropin. Central hypothyroidism may be caused by pituitary disease or deficiency of thyrotropin-releasing hormone.

Hypothyroidism also may be caused by treatments for hyperthyroidism, such as radioiodine therapy or surgery. In addition, treatment for certain cancers, such as surgery for thyroid cancer and external-beam radiation therapy directed to the neck in order to treat patients with tumours of the lymph nodes of the neck (Hodgkin disease) or of the larynx, may also cause hypothyroidism. Other causes include infiltrative diseases of the thyroid, severe iodine deficiency, and certain drugs (e.g., lithium carbonate, iodine, and iodine-containing drugs).

Like other thyroid diseases, hypothyroidism is more common in women than men. The onset is usually gradual, taking several years for notable symptoms and signs to develop. However, it may be abrupt, taking only a few months to develop. Abrupt onset of hypothyroidism occurs most commonly after radioiodine treatment for hyperthyroidism. In some cases, hypothyroidism is very mild and is difficult to recognize because it causes few symptoms. In these patients, the condition may be attributed to aging. In other cases, hypothyroidism can be very severe, especially if it is allowed to progress untreated for months or years.

The clinical manifestations of hypothyroidism are characterized by slowing of most body functions. Neuromuscular symptoms include slowing of thought, speech, and action, lethargy and fatigue, sleepiness, muscle aches and weakness, and slow reflexes. Other common symptoms are dry skin and hair, decreased perspiration, puffy eyes, cold intolerance, deepening of the voice, decreased appetite but a tendency to gain weight, constipation, and irregular menstrual periods and increased menstrual blood flow in women. Cardiac contractility and heart rate decrease as a result of hypothyroidism. In later stages of thyroid deficiency, fluid may accumulate around the heart, causing a condition known as pericardial effusion. Hypothyroidism also raises serum cholesterol concentrations. In very young children hypothyroidism causes intellectual disability, and in children of all ages it causes growth retardation.

In rare cases, hypothyroidism is life-threatening. This is called myxedema coma. The term *myxedema* refers to thickening of the skin and other organs due to the accumulation of glycosaminoglycans (large carbohydrates and proteins) associated with low serum thyroid hormone concentrations. Myxedema coma is characterized by nonresponsiveness, low body temperature (hypothermia), and respiratory depression. This condition is commonly precipitated by intake of sedating drugs, cold exposure, or infection and occurs most often in elderly women.

Hypothyroidism in infants, though treatable, can occasionally lead to severe intellectual disability and growth retardation leading to dwarfism.

Normal fetal development requires both maternally and fetally produced thyroid hormone. In the first 12 weeks of gestation the fetus is dependent on maternal thyroid hormone. At about 12 weeks the fetal thyroid gland begins to function, although some maternal thyroid hormone crosses the placenta to reach the fetal circulation. The most-severe impairment of fetal mental and skeletal development, known as cretinism, occurs when both mother and fetus have thyroid deficiency. This tends to occur more often in regions of the world where severe iodine deficiency is a problem. Cretinism also occurs in infants who have little or no thyroid tissue, especially if the hypothyroidism is not recognized very soon after birth. The ability to prevent cretinism by prompt treatment has led to routine screening for hypothyroidism in newborns.

The diagnosis of hypothyroidism is confirmed by measuring serum thyroxine (the thyroid hormone produced in greatest quantity) and thyrotropin. Measurements of free serum hormone detect hormones that are not bound to proteins in the blood and therefore circulate freely through the body. Measurements of total serum hormone detect hormones that are bound to protein in the blood and hormones that are free. These measurements are significant because free thyroid hormones are metabolically

Australia's shortest competitive male bodybuilder, David Clarke, stands at 147 cm (4 feet 10 inches) tall. He is pictured here in front of his brother Paul at North Beach on Nov. 10, 2007, in Perth. Paul Kane/ Getty Images

active, whereas hormones bound to proteins are not. In hypothyroidism the usual findings are low serum total and free thyroxine concentrations and high serum thyrotropin concentrations. An exception is that serum thyrotropin concentrations are normal or low in patients with hypothyroidism caused by hypothalamic or pituitary disease. Some patients have high serum thyrotropin concentrations but normal serum concentrations of thyroxine and triiodothyronine (the thyroid hormone normally produced in the lowest quantity). This is known as subclinical hypothyroidism, and these patients have few or no symptoms and signs of hypothyroidism.

Patients with hypothyroidism should be treated with thyroxine in doses sufficient to raise serum thyroxine concentrations and lower serum thyrotropin concentrations. This treatment normalizes serum thyroxine and thyrotropin concentrations and is usually sufficient to reverse the symptoms and signs of hypothyroidism in patients of all ages. In newborn infants, treatment with thyroxine is initiated based on measurements of thyrotropin and thyroxine in blood that is obtained from the infant a few days after birth. Prompt treatment results in normal development.

MEDULLARY THYROID CARCINOMA

Medullary thyroid carcinoma is a tumour of the parafollicular cells (C cells) of the thyroid gland. It occurs both sporadically and predictably, affecting multiple members of families who carry gene mutations associated with the disease. In some families medullary thyroid carcinomas are the only tumours that appear, whereas in other families medullary thyroid carcinomas are one component of MEN2.

Medullary thyroid carcinomas are moderately malignant tumours that invade nearby tissues in the neck and spread to distant organs, such as the lungs and liver. A characteristic feature of these tumours is hypercalcitoninemia. Calcitonin normally functions to lower the concentration of calcium in the blood when it rises above the normal value. However, despite marked increases in serum calcitonin concentrations, patients with medullary thyroid carcinoma do not have low serum calcium concentrations (hypocalcemia), because their tissues are resistant to calcitonin.

Myxedema

Myxedema is a physiological reaction to hypothyroidism. It can be brought about by removal of the thyroid for any cause, by a cessation of function of the gland, or simply by glandular atrophy. The changes come on gradually: enlarged tongue; thickened skin with underlying fluid causing puffiness, particularly in the face around the eyelids and in the hands; drowsiness; apathy; sensitivity to cold; failure to menstruate (amenorrhea) or excessive menstrual bleeding (menorrhagia); cardiac enlargement; and lowering of the basal metabolic rate. The outlook for recovery, when treatment is with dessicated thyroid, is excellent. Therapy must be maintained permanently.

Other endocrine glands may be affected by the shortage of thyroid hormone: the gonadotropins, adrenocorticotropin, and growth hormone may be decreased. Ovarian dysfunction in myxedema is different in the primary and secondary types. In the former, menstrual flow may be more frequent, prolonged, and excessive. In the latter, if associated losses of gonadotropins are present, the menses cease. In the male, sexual activity and sperm production decrease. Fertility is reduced in both sexes. Myxedema may also cause delayed sexual maturation (which can be corrected by thyroid replacement), but sexual precocity can also occur. At times, the myxedema is accompanied by permanent primary hypofunction of the adrenal cortices (Addison disease; also called Schmidt syndrome).

Plummer Disease

Plummer disease (or toxic multinodular goitre) is a thyroid condition characterized by goitre, firm thyroid nodules, and hyperthyroidism. It is characterized by goitre, firm thyroid nodules, and hyperthyroidism. Plummer disease, which usually occurs in older people, is of unknown etiology. Its symptoms resemble those of hyperthyroidism with swelling of the thyroid gland.

Typically, persons affected by Plummer disease develop a goitre many years before the onset of symptoms of hyperthyroidism. Most patients are over age 50 before the characteristic accelerated heart rate and other cardiac conditions appear. Unlike Graves disease, Plummer disease seldom causes bulging of the eyes. Swelling of the thyroid gland may obstruct breathing or swallowing, requiring surgery to remove the excess tissue. The cardiac symptoms may result in congestive heart failure. In the absence of obstruction or cosmetic reasons for removing the gland, the goitre may be treated with drugs that block thyroid activity or with radioactive iodine therapy. However, the multiple thyroid nodules characteristic of the disease may raise suspicion of cancer, necessitating surgical excision of the gland.

Riedel Thyroiditis

Riedel thyroiditis (also called struma fibrosa, or ligneous thyroiditis) is an extremely rare form of chronic inflammation of the thyroid gland, in which the glandular tissues assume a densely fibrous structure, interfering with production of thyroid hormone and compressing the adjacent trachea and esophagus. The thyroid becomes enlarged, often asymmetrically, to form a firm, hard mass of scar tissue that may be confused with cancer of the thyroid. Other organs may also be involved, including the parotid (salivary) glands, the lungs, and the bile ducts of the liver. The fibrosis may also spread beyond the thyroid to surrounding tissues. The cause of the disease, which occurs most commonly in middle-aged and older individuals, is unknown. Treatment is largely symptomatic and may include thyroid replacement if hypothyroidism occurs. Surgery to remove the affected tissue may also be needed to relieve pressure on surrounding organs.

Sheehan Syndrome

Sheehan syndrome (postpartum pituitary necrosis) is an insufficiency of pituitary hormones (hypopituitarism) that is caused by the destruction of cells of the anterior pituitary gland by oxygen starvation, usually at the time of childbirth. The condition may also result from septic shock, burn shock, or a massive hemorrhage. Once the most common cause of hypopituitarism in women, Sheehan syndrome has become less common with improvements in obstetric practice.

In women giving birth, damage to the anterior pituitary may result from a drop in blood pressure caused by blood loss during and after delivery. The hypophyseal arteries, which supply the pituitary gland, constrict, temporarily cutting off the blood supply to the gland and killing some of its tissue. As long as at least 30 percent of the gland continues to function, no insufficiency of pituitary hormones will occur. Clinical manifestations of the syndrome include inability to produce milk, loss of axillary and pubic body hair, and failure to resume menstruation. Lifelong hormone replacement with estrogen, corticosteroids, or thyroid hormone stimulating drugs are necessary to correct the condition, restoring ovulation and stimulating the secretion of estrogenic hormones.

Thyroid Tumour

Thyroid tumours can be benign (adenomas) or malignant (cancers). Thyroid tumours are very common, and their frequency of occurrence increases with age. In the United States they are detected by physical examination in approximately 5 percent of the adult population and by ultrasound in approximately 40 percent of the adult population. In contrast, thyroid cancer is relatively rare. Only about 0.5 percent of all cancer deaths occur from thyroid cancer. The peak incidence of thyroid cancer occurs at about 50 years of age, and women are affected about three times as often as men.

Most thyroid tumours are adenomas, which have a wide variation of cellular patterns. Most of the tumours have well-developed follicles. Thus, they are collectively known as follicular adenomas. Most thyroid adenomas do not take up iodine or produce thyroid hormone. However, the main manifestation of a benign or malignant thyroid tumour is a painless mass in the neck.

The diagnosis of a nodule is confirmed by ultrasound. The only reliable way to distinguish between benign and malignant nodules is by fine-needle aspiration (removal) of cells, the characteristics of which are examined under a microscope by a pathologist. However, sometimes this distinction can be made only by study of the entire nodule.

The Chernobyl nuclear power plant disaster of 1986 in what is now the country of Ukraine has had serious and long-lasting effects on local crops, livestock, and people due to leaking radioactive gases. In this 2004 photo taken at a Kiev hospital, a young woman is having her thyroid checked by sonogram as part of an epidemiologic research program. Thyroid cancer is mostly being found among children. Patrick Landmann/Getty Images

Typically, 95 percent of nodules prove to be benign and 5 percent prove to be malignant. The benign nodules can be left alone. They enlarge only slightly, if at all, with time and can be removed surgically if they become bothersome to the patient. Malignant nodules, along with the entire thyroid gland, should be removed surgically to avoid potential metastasis (spread) to other sites of the body.

Most thyroid cancers are composed of mature-looking thyroid cells and grow very slowly. There are four types of thyroid cancer: papillary carcinoma, which accounts for about 90 percent of cases, and follicular carcinoma, anaplastic carcinoma, and medullary carcinoma, which together account for the remaining 10 percent of cases. Papillary and follicular carcinomas are very slow-growing tumours, and, while they can spread to lymph nodes in the neck, the lungs, or elsewhere, most patients are cured by a combination of surgery, radioactive iodine therapy, and thyroid hormone therapy. The only established risk factors for papillary carcinoma are external-beam radiation to the head and neck region and exposure to radioactive iodine in infants and children. In contrast to papillary and follicular carcinomas, anaplastic carcinomas are highly malignant and rapidly fatal. Medullary carcinomas are somewhat more malignant than papillary or follicular carcinomas.

DISEASES OF THE PARATHYROID GLANDS

Diseases of the parathyroid glands, similar to those of the thyroid, are characterized by either increased or decreased parathormone secretion. Increased parathormone secretion is known as hyperparathyroidism, whereas parathormone deficiency is called hypoparathyroidism.

HYPERPARATHYROIDISM

Hyperparathyroidism is an abnormal increase in the secretion of parathormone by one or more parathyroid glands. Hyperparathyroidism may be primary or secondary. In primary hyperparathyroidism, one or more parathyroid glands produces excessive amounts of parathormone. This causes an increase in serum calcium concentrations by stimulating the breakdown of bone and by increasing calcium reabsorption by the kidneys. In secondary (compensatory) hyperparathyroidism, the parathyroid glands become overactive in an attempt to compensate for low serum calcium concentrations. Secondary hyperparathyroidism occurs most often in patients with vitamin D deficiency or chronic kidney disease.

Primary hyperparathyroidism is most often caused by an adenoma (a benign tumour) of one parathyroid gland. The adenoma produces and secretes an excessive amount of parathormone largely independent of the serum calcium concentration. The cause of parathyroid gland tumours is not known. About 10 percent of patients have primary hyperplasia (abnormal increase in the number of cells) of all the parathyroid glands. Primary parathyroid hyperplasia can occur as a result of the familial disorder MEN1. In rare cases the cause of hyperparathyroidism is attributed to parathyroid carcinoma (a malignant tumour).

Primary hyperparathyroidism is a relatively common disorder and is usually detected when serum calcium is measured as part of a routine health examination. Most patients have mild hypercalcemia (increased serum calcium concentration), although there are some patients who have no symptoms at all. There are also other patients who have nonspecific symptoms, such as fatigue, weakness, depression, and loss of appetite. Patients with more-severe hypercalcemia may have nausea, vomiting, weight loss, constipation, bone pain, and more-marked weakness and depression. About 20 percent of cases are detected because patients develop kidney stones, and about 1 to 2 percent of cases are detected because the patient has symptomatic osteoporosis (loss of bone). In rare cases, patients have a severe form of osteoporosis called osteitis fibrosa cystica, in which there is intense local resorption of bone that results in the formation of cystlike spaces within the bones that are filled with fibrous tissue.

Secondary hyperparathyroidism may be caused by thiazide diuretic drugs (used to treat hypertension) and lithium carbonate (used to treat bipolar disorder). In some cases, serum calcium and serum parathormone concentrations are high as a result of a disorder called familial hypocalciuric hypercalcemia (familial benign hypercalcemia). This disorder is caused by a mutation in the calcium receptor gene that reduces the ability of calcium to inhibit parathormone secretion. In most patients with this disorder, serum calcium and parathormone concentrations are only minimally elevated.

Patients with primary hyperparathyroidism with symptoms of hypercalcemia, kidney stones, or bone disease are treated by surgical removal of the tumour (or most of the hyperplastic tissue). The most appropriate treatment of patients with asymptomatic hyperparathyroidism is less clear. Many of these patients remain symptom-free: their serum calcium concentrations do not increase, and their bone density does not decrease. Thus, one alternative is to monitor the patient from year to year, periodically measuring serum calcium and bone density, deciding to treat the patient only when the condition becomes more severe. Another alternative is to treat the patient with a bisphosphonate drug to prevent or decrease the rate of bone loss.

In patients who have acute marked symptoms of hypercalcemia, fluids are administered intravenously as a way to rapidly lower serum calcium concentrations. If that is not effective, a bisphosphonate drug, such as pamidronate or zoledronate, is administered intravenously to reduce hypercalcemia.

HYPOPARATHYROIDISM

Hypoparathyroidism is characterized by the inadequate secretion of parathormone. It can be due to decreased secretion of parathormone or, less often, to decreased action of parathormone (pseudohypoparathyroidism). In either case, hypoparathyroidism results in decreased mobilization of calcium from bone, decreased reabsorption of calcium by kidney tubule cells, decreased absorption of calcium by the gastrointestinal tract, and increased reabsorption of phosphate by kidney tubule cells. This abnormal pattern of calcium and phosphate regulation results in low serum calcium concentrations (hypocalcemia) and high serum phosphate concentrations.

The symptoms of hypoparathyroidism are the result of low serum calcium concentrations. Most prominent is muscular cramping and twitching, exemplified most dramatically by carpopedal (wrist and foot) spasms. These include painful contractions of the muscles of the arms and hands (and feet) in which the four fingers are rigidly extended while the thumb presses against the palm. This neuromuscular excitability can progress to generalized convulsions. Other common symptoms are a sensation of numbness and tingling around the mouth and in the hands and feet. Patients with chronic hypocalcemia may develop cataracts and calcification in the basal ganglia of the brain, which in turn can cause symptoms of parkinsonism. Patients who have pseudohypoparathyroidism may have skeletal abnormalities, including a short neck and extremities and shortened metacarpal bones, and may have abnormal physical features, characterized primarily by a rounded face.

Hypoparathyroidism is a rare disorder. Indeed, the most common cause is inadvertent removal of the parathyroid glands during thyroid gland surgery. In some cases, hypoparathyroidism will occur spontaneously as the result of an autoimmune disorder. In these patients, hypoparathyroidism is often only one component of a multiple endocrine deficiency syndrome. Other causes of hypoparathyroidism are iron deposition in the parathyroid glands (in patients with iron storage disorders), magnesium deficiency (usually in alcoholic patients), congenital absence of the parathyroid glands, and a mutation in the calcium receptor of the parathyroid glands that increases the ability of calcium to inhibit parathormone secretion. Most patients with pseudohypoparathyroidism have a genetic defect in which the action of parathormone on its target cells in the bones and kidneys is defective.

Other causes of hypocalcemia include vitamin D deficiency, vitamin D resistance, severe inflammation of the pancreas (pancreatitis), and, most common of all, severe kidney failure. All these disorders result in secondary (compensatory) hyperparathyroidism.

Patients with symptomatic hypocalcemia can be treated with intravenous administration of calcium salts. Long-term treatment consists of oral administration of vitamin D or calcitriol and of calcium salts. Serum calcium must be measured periodically to be certain that treatment is effective and that neither hypocalcemia nor hypercalcemia is present.

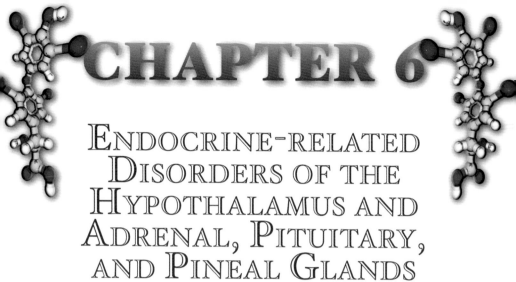

CHAPTER 6

ENDOCRINE-RELATED DISORDERS OF THE HYPOTHALAMUS AND ADRENAL, PITUITARY, AND PINEAL GLANDS

D iseases and disorders of the hypothalamus, the adrenal glands, and the pituitary gland are often complex in nature. Indeed, because these organs communicate via the hypothalmic-pituitary-adrenal axis, in which hormone secretion is governed by feedback loops involving each organ, disease in one organ frequently impacts the function of the other two.

An important coordinated function of these glands is the regulation of stress response. Under normal conditions, the release of corticotropin-releasing hormone from the hypothalamus stimulates the secretion of adrenocorticotropin from the anterior pituitary gland. Adrenocorticotropin then acts on the adrenal glands, prompting them to release the stress-mitigating, anti-inflammatory hormone cortisol. Its release in turn inhibits further release of corticotropin-releasing hormone from the hypothalamus. Hence, any disruption in hypothalamic, pituitary, or adrenal function can alter the body's ability to respond to stress, including physical and emotional stress. In addition, each organ is susceptible to a wide variety of diseases and disorders, which may be caused by genetic or environmental factors.

ENDOCRINE DISORDERS OF THE ADRENAL GLAND

Diseases of the adrenal glands may be divided into those of the medulla and those of the cortex. The only known disease of the adrenal medulla is pheochromocytoma, a type of tumour that was discussed previously. In contrast, the adrenal cortex is susceptible to multiple diseases and disorders, among which are several well-characterized conditions. Diseases of the adrenal cortex manifest in ways typical of classical endocrine dysfunction: as hyperfunction (excessive secretion of adrenocortical hormones) or hypofunction (insufficient secretion of these hormones). In the context of the adrenocortical hormones, the latter is also known as Addison disease.

Adrenocortical hyperfunction may be congenital or acquired. Congenital hyperfunction is always due to hyperplasia (enlargement) of both adrenal glands, whereas acquired hyperfunction may be due to either an adrenal tumour or hyperplasia. Congenital adrenal hyperplasia, also known as adrenogenital syndrome, is a disorder in which there is an inherited defect in one of the enzymes needed for the production of cortisol. Excessive amounts of adrenal androgens must be produced to overcome the block in cortisol production. In female infants this results in masculinization with pseudohermaphroditism (anomalous development of genital organs), whereas in male infants it results in premature sexual development (sexual precocity). Acquired adrenocortical hyperfunction is manifested by either cortisol excess (Cushing syndrome), androgen excess, or aldosterone excess (primary aldosteronism).

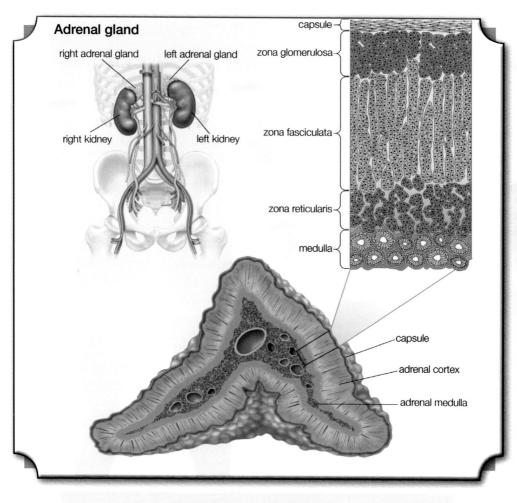

Human adrenal gland. Encyclopædia Britannica, Inc.

Addison Disease

Addison disease (also called hypocortisolism, or adrenal insufficiency) is a rare disorder defined by destruction of the outer layer of the adrenal glands, the hormone-producing organs located just above the kidneys. Addison disease is rare because it only occurs when at least 90 percent of the adrenal cortex is destroyed.

In the mid-19th century when the English physician Thomas Addison first described the clinical features of the disease, the destruction of the adrenal cortex was attributed to tuberculosis. Today, worldwide, tuberculosis is still a cause of the disease. However, in developed countries about 70 percent of cases result from an autoimmune reaction—an inappropriate attack by the immune system against, in this case, the adrenal glands. Autoimmune destruction of the adrenal glands is sometimes inherited as part of a multiple endocrine deficiency syndrome.

Other causes of Addison disease are infectious diseases, including fungal infections (e.g., histoplasmosis) and viral infections (e.g., cytomegalovirus). Tuberculosis and fungal infections typically result in the calcification of the adrenal glands. Noninfectious causes of Addison disease include adrenal hemorrhage or infarction, metastatic cancer, congenital adrenal hyperplasia, bilateral adrenalectomy (surgical removal of both adrenal glands), and drugs such as ketoconazole (an antifungal drug that inhibits steroid synthesis) and mitotane (a derivative of the insecticide DDT that causes adrenocortical suppression). Addison disease may also occur as a result of diseases of the pituitary gland, which cause adrenocorticotropin deficiency, or diseases of the hypothalamus, which cause corticotropin-releasing hormone deficiency.

The adrenal cortex produces numerous hormones called corticosteroids, which are involved in important functions of the body such as regulation of metabolism, blood pressure, and sodium and potassium levels. Damage to the cortex disrupts the production of two of these hormones, cortisol and aldosterone, leading to a variety of symptoms, including weakness, darkening of the skin and mucous membranes, poor appetite, weight loss, low blood pressure, gastrointestinal upset, and craving for salt or salty foods.

The symptoms of Addison disease increase in intensity over time and eventually (after several months) lead to acute adrenal insufficiency, known as adrenal crisis. Adrenal crisis is characterized by fever, vomiting, diarrhea, and a precipitous fall in blood pressure. The patient may go into shock and die unless he or she is treated vigorously with an intravenous saline solution and with cortisol or other glucocorticoids. Adrenal crisis may occur in individuals with no previous evidence of adrenal disease and may be provoked by physical stress, such as trauma or illness. The most common cause of adrenal crisis is bilateral adrenal hemorrhage, which can occur in newborn infants and in adults, especially in those who are treated with anticoagulant drugs (e.g., heparin or warfarin).

Addison disease, if undiagnosed, is fatal. The onset is often gradual and the symptoms may be nonspecific. Most patients with the condition have deficiencies in aldosterone and cortisol and therefore have decreased serum sodium concentrations (hyponatremia) and increased serum potassium concentrations (hyperkalemia). In contrast, deficiencies in aldosterone are not found in patients with diseases of the hypothalamus or the pituitary gland.

Replacement therapy with cortisol (hydrocortisone) and fluorohydrocortisone (a mineralocorticoid used as a substitute for aldosterone) will control the symptoms of the disease, but the treatment must be continued throughout life. For some patients, salt tablets can be given in place of a mineralocorticoid. Because aldosterone is poorly absorbed from the intestine, it is not used to treat adrenal deficiency. In addition, patients with Addison disease must take additional doses of cortisol during periods of acute illness or injury. Patients who receive adequate treatment can live normal lives.

BARTTER SYNDROME

Bartter syndrome (or potassium wasting syndrome) is a rare disorder affecting the kidneys. It is characterized primarily by the excessive excretion of potassium in the urine. Because increased production of aldosterone is a central finding of Bartter syndrome, the disorder is recognized as a form of secondary hyperaldosteronism.

The onset of Bartter syndrome is usually in infancy or in childhood and may result in short stature and intellectual disability. Bartter syndrome can be divided into three main categories: neonatal Bartter syndrome, appearing in utero between 24 and 30 weeks of gestation; classic Bartter syndrome, appearing in infancy or early childhood; and Gitelman syndrome, appearing in late childhood or in adulthood.

Neonatal Bartter syndrome has two types, which are clinically indistinguishable. Type 1 is caused by mutation of the gene called *SLC12A1* (solute carrier family 12, member 1), and type 2 is caused by mutation of the gene *KCNJ1* (potassium inwardly rectifying channel, subfamily J, member 1). Both genes normally work to maintain homeostasis of sodium and potassium concentrations.

Classic Bartter syndrome, or type 3, is caused by mutation in the gene *CLCNKB* (chloride channel Kb), which functions in chloride and sodium reabsorption in the kidney tubules. Mutations underlying classic Bartter syndrome result in the loss of function of the encoded protein. This leads to excessive excretion of sodium in the urine. Infantile Bartter syndrome with sensorineural deafness, or type 4, is caused by a combination of variations in *CLCNKB* and *CLCNKA* (chloride channel Ka) or by variation of the gene called *BSND* (Bartter syndrome, infantile, with sensorineural deafness).

Gitelman syndrome is caused by mutations in *SLC12A3* (solute carrier family 12, member 3). This gene encodes a protein that specializes in the transport of sodium and chloride into the kidney tubules and thereby mediates the reabsorption of these electrolytes and maintains electrolyte homeostasis.

Bartter syndrome is diagnosed primarily on findings of increased potassium levels in the urine and increased concentrations of aldosterone and renin in the blood serum. Diagnosis of Gitelman syndrome is based on findings similar to Bartter syndrome, as well as on hypomagnesemia, or abnormally low serum concentrations of magnesium, and hypocalciuria, or decreased levels of calcium in the urine.

Hypokalemia (low potassium levels in the blood) may be treated with potassium supplements, and additional supplements may be used to maintain sodium and other electrolyte concentrations. Despite treatment, some patients may develop kidney failure.

CUSHING SYNDROME

Cushing syndrome is a disorder caused by overactivity of the adrenal cortex. If caused by a tumour of the pituitary gland, it is called Cushing disease.

In 1932 American neurosurgeon Harvey Cushing described the clinical findings that provided the link between specific physical characteristics (e.g., abnormal obesity of the face and trunk) and a specific type of pituitary tumour. This pituitary disorder became known as Cushing syndrome. However, it later became clear that many patients with similar symptoms and signs did not have a pituitary tumour. Thus, the term *Cushing syndrome* has been modified to refer to all patients with the classic symptoms and signs of the condition, regardless of the cause, while the term *Cushing disease* is restricted to patients in whom the symptoms and signs are caused by an adrenocorticotropic hormone-secreting pituitary tumour. Among patients with spontaneously occurring Cushing syndrome, about 70 percent have Cushing disease.

Although Cushing syndrome is a relatively rare disease, it is four times as common in women as in men and may appear during or just following pregnancy. It can occur at any age but most typically appears during the third to sixth decades of life.

Cushing syndrome is caused by the excessive secretion of cortisol by the adrenal cortex. In general, anything that increases the adrenal gland's secretion of glucocorticoid hormones will cause Cushing syndrome, including adrenal tumours and overproduction of adrenocorticotropin. Excess adrenocorticotropin may result from pituitary tumours (Cushing disease), as in Cushing's first group of symptomatic patients, or from inappropriate production of the hormone by other tissues that do not ordinarily make adrenocorticotropin (ectopic corticotropin syndrome).

Tumours of the adrenal cortex that give rise to Cushing syndrome may be benign or malignant. These types of tumours occur in about 10 percent of patients. Adrenocorticotropin-producing tumours of non-endocrine tissues that do not normally produce adrenocorticotropin occur in about 20 percent of patients. Tumours of the hypothalamus in the brain or tumours of other tissues that produce corticotropin-releasing hormone rarely cause the disease. Iatrogenic Cushing syndrome is far more common than any of the disorders described above and is caused by the therapeutic administration of high doses of glucocorticoids, usually in the form of prednisone, prednisolone, or dexamethasone.

Glucocorticoid drugs are commonly used for the treatment of chronic inflammatory and allergic disorders and for immunosuppression.

For the most part, the symptoms and signs of Cushing syndrome are caused by excess cortisol. However, depending on the cause, there may also be symptoms and signs of excess mineralocorticoids, androgens, or adrenocorticotropin. The most common symptoms and signs of excess levels of cortisol in the body are obesity, facial plethora (facial redness), violaceous abdominal striae (purple or bluish stripes on the abdomen), thinning of the skin that leads to spontaneous bruising, muscle weakness and wasting, back pain, osteopenia and osteoporosis, depression and other psychological symptoms, hypertension, and menstrual disturbances (oligomenorrhea and amenorrhea) in women. Weight gain associated with excess cortisol occurs in a peculiar distribution, with fat accumulation confined to the central body areas, such as the abdomen, back, and buttocks. In contrast, the extremities, such as the arms and legs, are thin as a result of loss of muscle mass. Excess fat deposits also occur in the cheeks, giving rise to a "moon face," as well as in the anterior neck, producing a "dewlap," or in the upper back, producing a "buffalo hump." Excess levels of cortisol also cause increased gluconeogenesis (formation of glucose from noncarbohydrate sources) and decreased insulin sensitivity, which may give rise to diabetes mellitus. Patients with adrenal cancer may have increased production of adrenal androgens that cause excess hair growth (hirsutism), virilization (characterized by frontal balding and deepening of the voice), and menstrual abnormalities in women. Patients with ectopic corticotropin syndrome may have hyperpigmentation and mineralocorticoid excess.

A diagnosis of Cushing syndrome is often confirmed by the presence of high levels of cortisol in the serum, saliva, or urine. The different causes of Cushing syndrome are distinguished from one another by measurements of serum adrenocorticotropin and serum cortisol concentrations before and after the administration of dexamethasone. If the production of excess cortisol is caused by Cushing disease (a pituitary tumour), cortisol production decreases after the administration of dexamethasone, whereas cortisol production will not decrease if the cause is an adrenal tumour. In addition, imaging studies directed toward identification of a pituitary or adrenal tumour or a tumour of nonendocrine tissue are used to distinguish the underlying cause of excess cortisol production.

Treatment of Cushing syndrome depends upon the specific cause. Many manifestations of the syndrome disappear when the cause of cortisol excess is removed. If the cause is from adrenocorticotropin or glucocorticoid treatment, remission occurs when treatment is discontinued. Pituitary tumours can be surgically removed in about 80 percent of patients with Cushing disease, and radiation therapy can be used to destroy the tumour if surgery is not an option or if the tumour cannot be removed completely. Adrenal tumours can be surgically removed, and patients with benign tumours are usually cured in this way. Complete surgical removal of an adrenal cancer is often impossible, and even when possible the patients are rarely cured. While these patients can be treated with drugs, such as ketoconazole and mitotane, to reduce cortisol secretion and slow tumour growth, most die within one to four years after diagnosis. Patients with ectopic adrenocorticotropin-producing tumours are treated by surgery, radiation, or chemotherapy. Occasionally, if the pituitary or nonendocrine tumour cannot be controlled, both adrenal glands may have to be removed. The ensuing adrenal insufficiency is treated in the same way as spontaneously occurring adrenal insufficiency. In patients with Cushing disease, bilateral adrenalectomy is sometimes followed by pituitary tumour growth and intense skin pigmentation, a combination known as Nelson syndrome.

Daily treatment with cortisol is essential if the adrenal glands have been completely removed and may also be necessary after partial removal of these glands. However, even when Cushing syndrome has been eradicated, some of the changes produced by the disorder may continue. For example, this is true of heart, blood vessel, and kidney changes and of osteoporosis.

HYPERALDOSTERONISM

Hyperaldosteronism is the increased secretion of the hormone aldosterone by the cells of the zona glomerulosa (the outer zone) of the adrenal cortex. The primary actions of aldosterone are to increase retention of salt and water and to increase excretion of potassium by the kidneys and to a lesser extent by the skin and intestine. Hyperaldosteronism may be classified as primary or secondary.

In 1955 American internist Jerome Conn described a form of high blood pressure (hypertension) associated with low serum potassium concentrations (hypokalemia) in patients who had a benign adenoma of the cells of the zona glomerulosa of the adrenal cortex. These patients had high serum aldosterone concentrations and increased urinary aldosterone excretion. In most patients, hypertension and hypokalemia disappeared when the tumour was removed. This disorder is called primary hyperaldosteronism, or primary aldosteronism, to distinguish it from secondary hyperaldosteronism, which is caused by disorders that result in loss of sodium and water from the body and decreased blood flow to the kidneys. Primary hyperaldosteronism also can result from hyperplasia of both adrenal glands.

Primary hyperaldosteronism is characterized by hypertension and low serum potassium concentrations, which can cause fatigue, muscle weakness, aches or cramps, and increased thirst and urination. In addition, patients may have headaches, numbness and tingling of the hands and feet, and disturbances in cardiac rhythm, including ventricular tachycardia.

Primary hyperaldosteronism is a rare cause of hypertension, accounting for fewer than 5 percent of cases. It is diagnosed by finding high concentrations of aldosterone in the serum and urine in the presence of low plasma renin activity. Other findings include hypokalemia and metabolic alkalosis (reduced acidity of the blood due to excessive excretion of acid from the body).

Hormonal and radiological studies can be used to distinguish primary hyperaldosteronism caused by an adrenal tumour from that caused by adrenal hyperplasia. The former is treated by surgery, whereas the latter is treated by antihypertensive drugs and by spironolactone, a drug that blocks the action of aldosterone on the kidney tubules.

Secondary hyperaldosteronism occurs as a consequence of activation of the normal physiologic mechanisms that maintain salt and water balance, blood volume, and blood flow to the kidneys. Under normal circumstances, the kidneys secrete the enzyme renin. When salt and water are lost—for example, as a result of diarrhea, persistent vomiting, or excessive perspiration—the production of renin is increased. Renin acts on a substance in the blood called angiotensinogen to produce angiotensin II, a peptide that stimulates aldosterone secretion from the adrenal gland. Increased renin production results in increased production of angiotensin and aldosterone. As aldosterone production increases, the kidneys are stimulated to reabsorb salt and water from the urine to correct deficits in serum electrolyte concentrations and in blood volume. Some diseases stimulate this same sequence of events. For example, congestive heart failure or cirrhosis of the liver can cause an effective decrease in blood pressure, and narrowing of a renal artery can cause a reduction in the flow of blood to a kidney. In all these situations, successful treatment of the primary disease leads to a restoration of normal renin, angiotensin, and aldosterone production. If treatment is unsuccessful, then drugs that block the action of aldosterone on the kidneys, such as spironolactone or eplerenone, can be given. Most patients with secondary hyperaldosteronism do not have hypertension or low serum potassium concentrations. The exception is patients with renal artery disease.

HYPOALDOSTERONISM

Hypoaldosteronism is characterized by abnormally low serum levels of aldosterone. Hypoaldosteronism nearly always arises as a result of disorders in which the adrenal glands are destroyed. However, there does exist a disease in which defective aldosterone synthesis and secretion from the zona glomerulosa in the adrenal gland occur in the presence of otherwise normal adrenocortical function.

Isolated aldosterone deficiency results in low serum sodium concentrations (hyponatremia), decreased extracellular (including plasma) volume, and high serum potassium concentrations (hyperkalemia). These biochemical changes cause weakness, postural hypotension (a decrease in blood pressure upon standing), salt craving, and heart block, which may be fatal. Hypoaldosteronism is often associated with mild to moderate kidney disease, especially in patients with diabetes mellitus. In patients with diabetes mellitus, hypoaldosteronism is caused by deficient production of renin by the kidneys that leads to decreased production of angiotensin II and therefore decreased secretion of aldosterone.

Other causes of hypoaldosteronism are rare and are primarily the result of enzymatic defects in the synthesis of aldosterone and resistance of the kidneys to the actions of aldosterone. In patients with hypoaldosteronism from these causes, renin production by the kidneys is increased. Treatment of hypoaldosteronism consists of the administration of salt or a potent synthetic mineralocorticoid such as fluorohydrocortisone (fludrocortisone). Orally administered aldosterone is ineffective because it is poorly absorbed by the body.

DISORDERS OF THE HYPOTHALAMUS AFFECTING ENDOCRINE FUNCTION

Injuries or diseases affecting the hypothalamus may produce symptoms of pituitary dysfunction or diabetes insipidus. In the latter disorder, the absence of vasopressin, which promotes the reabsorption of water in the kidneys, induces the rapid loss of water from the body through frequent urination. Hypothalamic disease can also cause insomnia and fluctuations in body temperature. In addition, the optic chiasm is particularly susceptible to pressure from expanding tumours or inflammatory masses in the hypothalamus or the pituitary gland. Pressure on the optic chiasm can result in visual defects or even blindness.

ADIPSIA

Adipsia (or hypodipsia) is a rare disorder characterized by the lack of thirst even in the presence of dehydration. In adipsia the brain's thirst centre, located in the hypothalamus, is damaged. People with adipsia have little or no sensation of thirst when they become dehydrated. These people must be instructed, even forced, to drink fluid at regular intervals.

A person becomes dehydrated when he or she is deprived of fluids or when losing excessive fluids from the body, such as from excessive perspiration, persistent vomiting, or diarrhea. In these circumstances, the volume of fluid in the circulation (plasma volume) is reduced and the serum concentration of solutes (osmolality) is therefore proportionately increased. The decrease in plasma volume and the proportional increase in serum osmolality serve as potent stimuli for the secretion of vasopressin, which then acts on the kidneys to promote retention of water. The most common causes of adipsia include lesions and other forms of trauma that affect the thirst centre in the hypothalamus.

FRÖHLICH SYNDROME

Fröhlich syndrome (or adiposogenital dystrophy) is a rare childhood metabolic disorder characterized by obesity, growth retardation, and retarded development of the genital organs. It is usually associated with tumours of the hypothalamus, causing increased appetite and depressed secretion of gonadotropin. The disease is named for Alfred Fröhlich, the Austrian neurologist who first described its typical pattern.

The syndrome occurs most frequently in boys and, because of the close association between the pituitary and the hypothalamus, may be associated with reduced pituitary function. Impaired vision sometimes results from impingement of the tumour on the optic nerve. Fröhlich syndrome is treated by removing the tumour and restricting diet until normal weight is achieved.

Many overweight children may appear to have the disorder because of the concurrence of obesity and retarded sexual development. These children have no endocrine disturbances, however, and they mature normally after delayed puberty.

DISEASES OF THE PITUITARY GLAND

Hypopituitarism refers to deficiencies of anterior and posterior pituitary hormones. The extent of deficiency varies from deficiency of a single hormone to deficiencies of all of them, known as panhypopituitarism. Tumours that secrete individual anterior pituitary hormones are recognized, and some of them secrete two anterior pituitary hormones, most often growth hormone and prolactin. Posterior pituitary tumours that secrete excess vasopressin or oxytocin do not occur.

GROWTH HORMONE DEFICIENCY

Growth hormone deficiency is one of the many causes of short stature and dwarfism. It results primarily from damage to the hypothalamus or to the pituitary gland during fetal development (congenital growth hormone deficiency) or following birth (acquired growth hormone deficiency). Growth hormone deficiency may also be caused by mutations in genes that regulate its synthesis and secretion. Affected genes include *PIT-1* (pituitary-specific transcription factor-1) and *POUF-1* (prophet of *PIT-1*). Mutations in these genes may also cause decreased synthesis and secretion of other pituitary hormones. In some cases, growth hormone deficiency is the result of growth hormone-releasing hormone deficiency, in which case growth hormone secretion may be stimulated by infusion of growth hormone-releasing hormone. In other cases, the somatotrophs themselves are incapable of producing growth hormone, or the hormone itself is structurally abnormal and has little growth-promoting activity. In addition, short stature and growth hormone deficiency are often found in children diagnosed with psychosocial dwarfism, which results from severe emotional deprivation. When children with this disorder are removed from the stressing, nonnurturing environment, their endocrine function and growth rate normalize.

Children with isolated growth hormone deficiency are normal in size at birth, but growth retardation becomes evident within the first two years of life. Radiographs (X-ray films) of the epiphyses (the growing ends) of bones show growth retardation in relation to the patient's chronological age. Although puberty is often delayed, fertility and delivery of normal children is possible in affected women.

Growth hormone deficiency is most often treated with injections of growth hormone. For decades, however, availability of the hormone was limited, because it was obtained solely from human cadaver pituitaries. In 1985 use of natural growth hormone was halted in the United States and several other countries because of the possibility that the hormone was contaminated with a type of pathogenic agent known as a prion, which causes a fatal condition called Creutzfeldt-Jakob disease. That same year, by means of recombinant DNA technology, scientists were able to produce a biosynthetic human form, which they called somatrem, thus assuring a virtually unlimited supply of this once-precious substance.

Children with growth hormone deficiency respond well to injections of recombinant growth hormone, often achieving near-normal height. However, some children, primarily those with the hereditary inability to synthesize growth hormone, develop antibodies in response to injections of the hormone. Children with short stature not associated with growth hormone deficiency may also grow in response to hormone injections, although large doses are often required.

A rare form of short stature is caused by an inherited insensitivity to the action of growth hormone. This disorder is known as Laron dwarfism and is characterized by abnormal growth hormone receptors, resulting in decreased growth hormone-stimulated production of IGF-1 and poor growth. Serum growth hormone concentrations are high because of the absence of the inhibitory action of IGF-1 on growth hormone secretion. Dwarfism may also be caused by insensitivity of bone tissue and other tissues to IGF-1, resulting from decreased function of IGF-1 receptors.

Growth hormone deficiency often persists into adulthood, although some people affected in childhood have normal growth hormone secretion in adulthood. Growth hormone deficiency in adults is associated with fatigue, decreased energy, depressed mood, decreased muscle strength, decreased muscle mass, thin and dry skin, increased adipose tissue, and decreased bone density. Treatment with growth hormone reverses some of these abnormalities but can cause fluid retention, diabetes mellitus, and high blood pressure (hypertension).

GROWTH HORMONE EXCESS

Excess growth hormone production is most often caused by a benign tumour (adenoma) of the somatotroph cells of the pituitary gland. In some cases, a tumour of the lung or of the pancreatic islets of Langerhans produces growth hormone-releasing hormone, which stimulates the somatotrophs to produce large amounts of growth hormone. In rare cases, ectopic production of growth hormone (production by tumour cells in tissues that do not ordinarily synthesize growth hormone) causes an excess of the hormone. Somatotroph tumours in children are very rare and cause excessive growth that may lead to extreme height (gigantism) and features of acromegaly.

Acromegaly

Acromegaly is a growth and metabolic disorder characterized by enlargement of the skeletal extremities. Patients with acromegaly have enlarged hands, feet, chin, and nose. The enlargement is due to the overgrowth of cartilage, muscle, subcutaneous tissue, and skin. Thus, patients with acromegaly have a prominent jaw, a large nose, and large hands and feet, as well as enlargement of most other tissues, including the tongue, liver, heart, and kidneys. The condition is the result of overproduction of pituitary growth hormone (somatotropin) after maturity, caused by a tumour of the pituitary gland. Acromegaly is

Londoner Mary Ann Bevan, seen here in November 1919 at age 45, developed the growth hormone disorder known as acromegaly as an adult. A. R. Coster/Hulton Archive/Getty Images

often associated with the abnormal growth in stature known as pituitary gigantism.

The onset of acromegaly is gradual. Acromegalic subjects may develop headache, excessive sweating, muscle weakness, high blood pressure, and even congestive heart failure, particularly when blood pressure becomes high. At times, excessive overgrowth of bone and cartilage involves the joints and causes pain. The bones may become thin and porous—a condition known as osteoporosis. Diabetes mellitus appears in 20 to 40 percent of acromegalic subjects because excess growth hormone blocks the action of insulin. If the pituitary tumour enlarges, it can cause visual-field defects, blindness or paralysis of the eye muscles, and can injure the posterior pituitary gland or the hypothalamus. Also, hemorrhage into the tumour can cause sudden loss of vision. Patients with acromegaly can also have arthritis and an increased risk of developing malignant tumours of the large intestine. Some somatotroph tumours also produce prolactin, which may cause abnormal lactation (galactorrhea).

Acromegaly may be treated by surgical removal of the pituitary tumour or destruction of it by X-ray irradiation or liquid nitrogen. Rarely, the pituitary tumour will cease to secrete growth hormone because of a spontaneous hemorrhage or a blockage of the blood supply. Decreases in acromegalic manifestations and amelioration of diabetes mellitus have followed therapy with female hormones—estrogen or medroxyprogesterone—which reduce the secretion of growth hormone. They can also be treated with drugs such as pegvisomant, which blocks the binding of growth hormone to its receptors, and synthetic long-acting analogues of somatostatin, which also inhibit the secretion of growth hormone. For those treated by pituitary surgery, irradiation, or other measures and for those who spontaneously develop deficits of gonadal, thyroidal, or adrenocortical hormones, replacement-hormone therapy is necessary.

Gigantism

Gigantism is an excessive growth in stature, well beyond the average for the individual's heredity and environmental conditions. Gigantism is caused by disease or disorder in the parts of the endocrine system that regulate growth and development. Androgen deficiency, for example, delays the closure of end plates, or epiphyses, of the long bones, which usually takes place when full growth is achieved. If the pituitary gland functions normally, producing appropriate amounts of growth hormone, while epiphyseal closure is delayed, the growth period of the bones will be prolonged. Gigantism associated with androgen deficiency is more frequent in men than in women and may be genetic.

Canadian circus performer Anna Haining Swan Bates, who was discovered by P.T. Barnum in 1862, is seen here c. 1870 with her parents, both of average stature. Bates stood over 2.3 metres (7 ½ feet) tall. Blank Archives/Hulton Archive/Getty Images

Another type of gigantism associated with endocrine disorder is pituitary gigantism, caused by hypersecretion of growth hormone, during childhood or adolescence, prior to epiphyseal closure. Pituitary gigantism is usually associated with a tumour of the pituitary gland. Acromegaly occurs if growth hormone continues to be produced in large volume after epiphyseal closure, and because most pituitary giants continue to produce growth hormone after they reach adulthood, the two conditions—gigantism and acromegaly—are often concurrent.

In pituitary gigantism, growth is gradual but continuous and consistent. The affected person, with bones in normal proportion, may attain a height of 2.4 metres (8 feet). Muscles may be well developed but later undergo some atrophy or weakening. The life span of pituitary giants is shorter than normal because of their greater susceptibility to infection and metabolic disorders. Treatment by surgery or irradiation of the pituitary gland curtails further growth, but stature cannot be reduced once gigantism has occurred.

HYPOPITUITARISM

Hypopituitarism is a deficiency of pituitary hormones caused by damage to the pituitary gland. Patients may have a deficiency of one or all pituitary hormones, including vasopressin (antidiuretic hormone), the hormone of the posterior pituitary gland that controls the excretion of urine. Deficiency of all pituitary hormones is known as panhypopituitarism. Pituitary hormone deficiencies can occur as a result of pituitary disease or hypothalamic disease, with deficiency of the hypothalamic hormones that stimulate the secretion of most pituitary hormones. The causes of hypopituitarism include pituitary and hypothalamic tumours, infections, postpartum pituitary hemorrhage (Sheehan syndrome), and surgery for secreting or nonsecreting pituitary tumours.

Pituitary Tumour

A pituitary tumour is the most common cause of enlargement of the sella turcica, the bone cavity in the head in which the pituitary gland is located. There are two general types of pituitary tumours—hormone secreting and nonsecreting. There are five types of hormone-secreting pituitary tumours, named according to the cells that produce the particular hormone. They are corticotropin-secreting tumours (corticotroph adenomas), which cause Cushing disease; gonadotropin-secreting tumours (gonadotroph adenomas), which can cause ovarian or testicular dysfunction; growth hormone- (somatotropin-) secreting tumours (somatotroph adenomas), which cause acromegaly and gigantism; prolactin-secreting tumours (prolactinomas), which cause galactorrhea (abnormal lactation), menstrual abnormalities, and infertility; and thyrotropin-secreting tumours (thyrotroph adenomas), which cause hyperthyroidism. Of these hormone-secreting tumours, those that secrete prolactin are the most common, followed by those that secrete adrenocorticotropin and growth hormone. Those that secrete sufficient gonadotropins or thyrotropin to cause clinically important hormonal abnormalities are rare. Occasional patients have a tumour that secretes two of these hormones, most often growth hormone and prolactin.

Hormone-secreting tumours constitute approximately 70 percent of pituitary tumours. The remaining 30 percent are nonsecreting. Nonsecreting tumours cause symptoms when they become large enough to interfere with the production of one or more pituitary hormones or expand upward out of the sella turcica to impinge on the optic nerves or other brain structures. Virtually all pituitary tumours are benign and hence are adenomas.

Treatment varies according to the type of tumour. Patients with corticotroph, gonadotroph, somatotroph, and thyrotroph adenomas and nonsecreting adenomas are usually treated by transsphenoidal resection of the tumour, in which the sella turcica is approached via the nose and the sphenoid sinus, which lies just below the sella turcica. Surgical resection is effective treatment for patients with these tumours, although the efficacy of surgery decreases with increasing tumour size. The mortality rate of transsphenoidal pituitary surgery is low (less than 1 percent), and fewer than 10 percent of patients have adverse effects from the operation, which include deficiencies of anterior pituitary hormones, diabetes insipidus (excretion of large volumes of urine caused by deficiency of vasopressin), postoperative infections, and leakage of cerebrospinal fluid into the nose.

Patients with prolactinomas, including those with visual symptoms from the tumour, are usually treated with dopamine agonist drugs such as bromocriptine and cabergoline. These drugs effectively decrease prolactin secretion and tumour size. In addition to surgery, patients with somatotroph adenomas can be treated with analogs of the hypothalamic hormone somatostatin, given by injection, which inhibit growth hormone secretion, or with a drug (pegvisomant) that blocks the action of growth hormone. Occasional patients with pituitary adenomas who have recurrences after surgery are treated with external-beam radiation. This is rarely used as initial treatment.

PINEAL TUMOUR

A pineal tumour is a mass of abnormal tissue arising in the pineal gland and occurring most often in children and young adults. Pineal tumours are rare. The most frequently occurring of these are germ cell tumours (germinomas and teratomas), which arise from embryonic remnants of germ cells (precursors of egg and sperm cells). Germ cell tumours are malignant and invasive and may be life-threatening. Tumours of the pinealocytes (the primary cell type of the pineal gland) also occur and vary in their potential for malignant change.

Pineal tumours may cause headache, vomiting, and seizures because of the increase in intracranial pressure that results from the enlarging tumour mass. Some patients may become hypogonadal with regression of secondary sex characteristics, whereas others may undergo precocious puberty because of secretion of human chorionic gonadotropin. Diabetes insipidus, which is characterized by excessive thirst and excessive production of very dilute urine, is frequently present and is usually due to tumour invasion of the hypothalamus. Invasion of the pituitary stalk may interfere with the inhibition of prolactin secretion by dopamine from the hypothalamus, resulting in high serum prolactin concentrations. Treatment consists of surgery and radiation therapy.

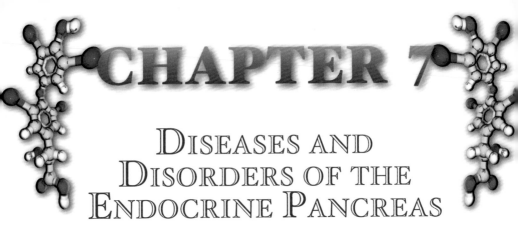

CHAPTER 7

DISEASES AND DISORDERS OF THE ENDOCRINE PANCREAS

The endocrine pancreas is the site of production of the hormones insulin and glucagon, which play central roles in glucose metabolism. Thus, a classic indication of disease in the endocrine pancreas is altered glucose homeostasis, which is apparent clinically as abnormally high or low levels of glucose in the blood. Such alterations in blood glucose levels typically arise from either a deficiency in insulin or a deficiency in tissue response to insulin (insulin facilitates the removal of glucose from the bloodstream). Both conditions can lead to diabetes mellitus, a disease that affects tens of millions of people worldwide.

ABNORMALITIES IN GLUCOSE METABOLISM

Abnormalities in glucose metabolism can be detected clinically by measuring the concentration of glucose in the blood. Two possible findings of such tests are hyperglycemia (elevated blood glucose levels) and hypoglycemia (reduced blood glucose levels), each of which is a reflection of abnormal glucose metabolism and hence is indicative of disease in the endocrine pancreas.

Hyperglycemia is an elevation of blood glucose concentrations above the normal range. It is the laboratory finding that establishes a diagnosis of diabetes mellitus. Hyperglycemia results from a decrease in the body's ability to utilize or store glucose after carbohydrates are ingested and from an increase in the production of glucose by the liver during the intervals between meals. It is caused by a decrease in the production of insulin, a decrease in the action of insulin, or a combination of the two abnormalities. Mild hyperglycemia causes no symptoms, but more severe hyperglycemia causes an increase in urine volume and thirst, fatigue and weakness, and increased susceptibility to infection. Extremely high blood glucose concentrations result in loss of blood volume, low blood pressure, and impaired central nervous system function (hyperglycemic coma).

Hypoglycemia is a reduction of the concentration of glucose in the blood below normal levels, commonly occurring as a complication of treatment for diabetes mellitus. In healthy individuals an intricate glucoregulatory system acts rapidly to counter hypoglycemia by reducing insulin production and mobilizing energy reserves from the fat and liver. When this regulatory system does not operate, disproportionately large amounts of insulin in the blood result in sudden drastic falls in circulating glucose.

The manifestations of hypoglycemia evolve in a characteristic pattern. Mild hypoglycemia—for example, blood glucose concentrations less than 55 mg per 100 ml (3 mmol/l)—causes hunger, fatigue, tremour, rapid pulse, and anxiety. These symptoms are known as sympathoadrenal symptoms because they are caused by activation of the sympathetic nervous system, including the adrenal medulla. Activation of the sympathetic nervous system increases blood glucose concentrations by mobilizing liver glycogen, which is the principal storage form of carbohydrate in liver and muscle. More severe hypoglycemia—for example, blood glucose concentrations less than 45 mg per

100 ml (2.5 mmol/l)—causes blurred vision, impaired thinking and consciousness, confusion, seizures, and coma. These symptoms are known as neuroglycopenic symptoms because they are indicative of glucose deprivation in the brain. Sympathoadrenal symptoms and neuroglycopenic symptoms are nonspecific and should be attributed to hypoglycemia only when relieved by either oral or intravenous administration of glucose.

The principal causes of hypoglycemia can be grouped into two categories: insulin-dependent and insulin-independent. Insulin-dependent hypoglycemia is caused by too much insulin (hyperinsulinemia), usually attributed to the intake of a sulfonylurea drug or to the presence of excess insulin in a patient with diabetes. Other, much less common causes of insulin-dependent hypoglycemia may include an insulin-secreting tumour of the islets of Langerhans or a tumour, usually of fibrous tissue, that secretes insulin-like growth factor 2 (IGF-2), which activates insulin receptors. Insulin-independent hypoglycemia is caused by disorders that result in impaired glucose mobilization during fasting (defects in gluconeogenesis or glycogenolysis). Impaired glucose mobilization may be caused by adrenal insufficiency, severe liver disease, glycogen storage disease, severe infections, and starvation. Insulin-dependent hypoglycemia is diagnosed by an inappropriately high serum insulin concentration when symptoms of hypoglycemia are present. Conversely, insulin-independent hypoglycemia is diagnosed by an inappropriately low serum insulin concentration when symptoms of hypoglycemia are present.

Many people have hypoglycemia-like symptoms three to five hours after a meal. However, few of these people have hypoglycemia when symptomatic, and their symptoms may not improve with the administration of glucose. Symptoms can often be controlled by eating small snacks every few hours, exercising regularly, and managing weight. A known cause of postmeal hypoglycemia is gastrectomy (removal of the stomach) or gastric bypass surgery for obesity, which results in rapid absorption of glucose into the blood, thereby triggering excessive insulin secretion and hypoglycemia.

DIABETES MELLITUS

Diabetes mellitus is a disorder of carbohydrate metabolism that is characterized by an impaired ability of the body to produce or respond to insulin. This in turn impairs the body's ability to maintain proper levels of glucose in the blood.

Diabetes is a major cause of morbidity and mortality, though these outcomes are not due to the immediate effects of the disorder. They are instead related to the diseases of large blood vessels (e.g., coronary heart disease), small blood vessels (e.g., renal vascular disease), and nerves that develop as a result of chronic diabetes mellitus.

CAUSES AND TYPES

Insulin's role in the body is to trigger cells to take up glucose so that the cells can use this energy-yielding sugar. Patients with diabetes may have dysfunctional beta cells in the islets of Langerhans, resulting in decreased insulin secretion, or their muscle and adipose cells may be resistant to the effects of insulin, resulting in a decreased ability of these cells to take up and metabolize glucose. In both cases, the levels of glucose in the blood increase, causing hyperglycemia. As glucose accumulates in the blood, excess levels of this sugar are excreted in the urine. Because of greater amounts of glucose in the urine, more water is excreted with it, causing an increase in urinary volume and frequency of urination as well as thirst. (The name *diabetes mellitus* refers to these symptoms: *diabetes*, from the Greek *diabainein*, meaning "to pass through," describes the copious urination, and *mellitus*, from the Latin meaning "sweetened with honey," refers to sugar in the urine.) Other symptoms of diabetes include itching, hunger, weight loss, and weakness. There are two major forms of the disease: type I, formerly referred to as insulin-dependent diabetes mellitus (IDDM) and juvenile-onset diabetes, and type II, formerly called non-insulin-dependent diabetes mellitus (NIDDM) and adult-onset diabetes.

Type I diabetes accounts for about 5 to 10 percent of cases of diabetes. Most patients with type I diabetes are children or adolescents, but about 20 percent are adults.

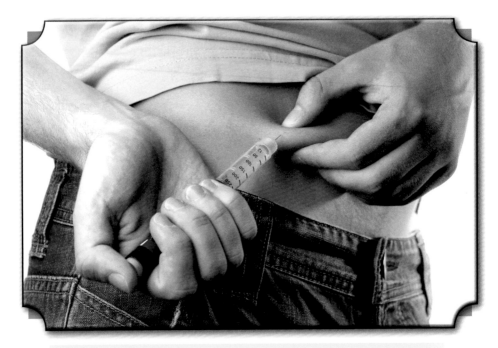

A patient with diabetes self-administers an injection of insulin. Canadian physician Frederick Grant Banting and his assistant Charles H. Best isolated the hormone in 1921. Shutterstock.com

Most patients present with symptoms of hyperglycemia, but some patients present with diabetic ketoacidosis, a clear indication that insulin secretion has significantly deteriorated. Type I diabetes is usually caused by autoimmune destruction of the islets of Langerhans of the pancreas. Patients with type I diabetes have serum antibodies to several components of the islets of Langerhans, including antibodies to insulin itself. The antibodies are often present for several years before the onset of diabetes, and their presence may be associated with a decrease in insulin secretion. Some patients with type I diabetes have genetic variations associated with the human leukocyte antigen (HLA) complex, which is involved in presenting antigens to immune cells and initiating the production of antibodies that attack the body's own cells (autoantibodies). However, the actual destruction of the islets of Langerhans is thought to be caused by immune cells sensitized in some way to components of islet tissue rather than to the production of autoantibodies. In general, 2 to 5 percent of children whose mother or father has type I diabetes will also develop type I diabetes.

Type II diabetes is far more common than type I diabetes, accounting for about 90 percent of all cases. Most patients with type II diabetes are adults, often older adults, but it can also occur in children and adolescents. Although the condition is linked to genetic factors, it is also strongly associated with environmental factors, and obesity in particular, in which case it may arise as a result of insulin resistance or insulin deficiency. In obese type II diabetes patients, insulin resistance manifests as higher-than-normal serum insulin concentrations. Some obese persons, however, are unable to produce sufficient amounts of insulin. This condition manifests as hyperglycemia, because the compensatory release of insulin that enables tissues to take up glucose from the blood is inadequate.

People with type II diabetes can control blood glucose levels through diet and exercise and, if necessary, by taking insulin injections or oral medications. If left uncontrolled, high blood glucose concentrations can lead to very severe and prolonged hyperglycemia and to marked polyuria (the passage of excessive volumes of urine), with the loss of a large volume of fluid and a very high serum osmolality. These factors place patients with type II diabetes at a high risk of developing central nervous system dysfunction and vascular collapse (hyperglycemia coma). Ketoacidosis is usually not a problem in patients with type II diabetes because they secrete enough insulin to restrain lipolysis. Patients with hyperglycemic coma should be treated aggressively with intravenous fluids and insulin.

DIAGNOSIS AND TREATMENT

Many people are unaware that they have diabetes. In the late 20th century, for example, it was estimated that more than 5 million of the 15.7 million American cases were undiagnosed. The disease is usually discovered when there are typical symptoms of increased thirst and urination and a clearly elevated blood sugar level. The diagnosis of diabetes is based on the presence of blood glucose concentrations equal to or greater than 126 mg per 100 ml (7.0 mmol/l) after an overnight fast or on the presence of blood glucose concentrations greater than 200 mg per 100 ml (11.1 mmol/l) in general. People with fasting blood glucose values between 110 and 125 mg per 100 ml (6.1 to 6.9 mmol/l) are diagnosed with a condition called impaired fasting glucose. Normal fasting blood glucose concentrations are less than 110 mg per 100 ml (6.1 mmol/l). Oral glucose tolerance tests, in which blood glucose is measured hourly for several hours after ingestion of a large quantity of glucose (usually 75 or 100 grams), are used in pregnant women to test for gestational diabetes. The criteria for diagnosing gestational diabetes are more stringent than the criteria for diagnosing other types of diabetes, which is a reflection of the presence of decreased blood glucose concentrations in healthy pregnant women as compared with nonpregnant women and with men.

The duration and severity of hyperglycemia can be assessed by measuring levels of advanced glycosylation end products (AGEs). AGEs are formed when hemoglobin molecules in red blood cells undergo glycosylation (binding to glucose), and the bound substances remain together until the red blood cell dies (red blood cells live approximately 120 days). AGEs are believed to inflict the majority of vascular damage that occurs in people with diabetes. A glycosylated hemoglobin called hemoglobin subtype A1c (HbA1c) is particularly useful in monitoring hyperglycemia and the efficacy of diabetes treatments.

All diabetes patients are put on diets designed to help them reach and maintain normal body weight, and they often are encouraged to exercise regularly, which enhances the movement of glucose into muscle cells and blunts the rise in blood glucose that follows carbohydrate ingestion. Patients are encouraged to follow a diet that is relatively low in fat and contains adequate amounts of protein. In practice about 30 percent of calories should come from fat, 20 percent from protein, and the remainder from carbohydrates, preferably from complex carbohydrates rather than simple sugars.

The total caloric content should be based on the patient's nutritional requirements for growth or for weight loss if the patient is obese. In overweight or obese patients with type II diabetes, caloric restriction for even just a few days may result in considerable improvement in hyperglycemia. In addition, weight loss, preferably combined with exercise, can lead to improved insulin sensitivity and even restoration of normal glucose metabolism.

Diabetics who are unable to produce insulin in their bodies receive regular injections of the hormone, which are often customized according to their individual and variable requirements. Modern human insulin treatments are based on recombinant DNA technology. Human insulin may be given as a form that is identical to the natural form found in the body, which acts quickly but transiently, or as a form that has been biochemically modified so as to prolong its action for up to 24 hours.

The optimal regimen is one that most closely mimics the normal pattern of insulin secretion, which is

Registered nurse Susan Eager (left), *who works for the Dominican Sisters Home Health Agency, a nonprofit that provides free home nursing care to patients with chronic diseases, checks the feet of patient Jane Awise at her home in Colorado. Awise suffers from severe diabetes.* John Moore/Getty Images a constant low level of insulin secretion plus a pulse of secretion after each meal. This can be achieved by administration of a long-acting insulin preparation once daily plus administration of a rapid-acting insulin preparation with or just before each meal. Patients also have the option of using an insulin pump, which allows them to control variations in the rate of insulin administration. A satisfactory compromise for some patients is twice-daily administration of mixtures of intermediate-acting and short-acting insulin. Patients taking insulin also may need to vary food intake from meal to meal, according to their level of activity. As exercise frequency and intensity increase, less insulin and more food intake may be necessary.

Research into other areas of insulin therapy include pancreas transplantation, beta cell transplantation, implantable mechanical insulin infusion systems, and the generation of beta cells from existing exocrine cells in the pancreas. Patients with type I diabetes have been treated by transplantation of the pancreas or of the islets of Langerhans.

There are several classes of oral drugs used to control blood glucose levels, including sulfonylureas, biguanides, and thiazolidinediones. Sulfonylureas, such as glipizide and glimepiride, are considered hypoglycemic agents because they stimulate the release of insulin from beta cells in the pancreas, thus reducing blood glucose levels. The most common side effect associated with sulfonylureas is hypoglycemia (abnormally low blood glucose levels), which occurs most often in elderly patients who have impaired liver or kidney function.

Biguanides, of which metformin is the primary member, are considered antihyperglycemic agents because they work by decreasing the production of glucose in the liver and by increasing the action of insulin on muscle and adipose tissues. A potentially fatal side effect of metformin is the accumulation of lactic acid in blood and tissues, often causing vague symptoms such as nausea and weakness.

Thiazolidinediones, such as rosiglitazone and pioglitazone, act by reducing insulin resistance of muscle and adipose cells and by increasing glucose transport into these tissues. These agents can cause edema (fluid accumulation in tissues), liver toxicity, and adverse cardiovascular events in certain patients. Furthermore, oral hypoglycemic agents lower mean blood glucose concentrations by only about 50–80 mg per 100 ml (2.8–4.4 mmol/l), and sensitivity to these drugs tends to decrease with time. There are also several other agents, including pramlintide, exenatide, and sitagliptin, that can be highly effective in the treatment of diabetes. Each of these drugs works by a unique mechanism to help regulate blood glucose levels.

All patients with diabetes mellitus, particularly those taking insulin, should measure blood glucose concentrations periodically at home, especially when they have symptoms of hypoglycemia. This is done by pricking a finger, obtaining a drop of blood, and using an instrument called a glucometer to measure the blood glucose concentration. Using this technology, many patients become skilled at evaluating their diabetes and making appropriate adjustments in therapy on their own initiative.

PANCREATIC CANCER

Pancreatic cancer is a disease characterized by abnormal growth of cells in the pancreas. Ninety-five percent of pancreatic cancers develop from the exocrine pancreas. The remaining 5 percent are often called neuroendocrine tumours or islet-cell cancers, which develop from endocrine cells.

SYMPTOMS AND CAUSES

The causes of pancreatic cancer vary and in many cases remain unknown. However, several factors have been identified that increase the risk of developing pancreatic cancer. The two most important of these factors are smoking, which is associated with about 30 percent of pancreatic tumours, and central obesity (accumulation of fat primarily around the abdomen), which can increase the risk of pancreatic cancer by as much as 70 percent in some postmenopausal women. In both men and women, central obesity is associated with increased levels of insulin and with disruption of normal endocrine and metabolic functions. However, the mechanism by which abnormally high insulin levels and dysfunctional metabolism in centrally obese individuals give rise to pancreatic cancer is unclear. A diet high in animal products, particularly animal fat, also increases cancer risk. Environmental factors, such as exposure to certain dyes, pesticides, and petroleum products, may increase the probability of developing pancreatic cancer as well.

Uncontrollable risk factors include age, sex—males are 30 percent more likely to develop cancers of the pancreas than are females—and illnesses such as diabetes mellitus and chronic pancreatitis. An estimated 10 percent of cases of pancreatic cancer are the result of inherited defects. Some of these cases arise in association with known genetic syndromes, such as Peutz-Jeghers syndrome and hereditary nonpolyposis colon cancer, whereas others are associated with familial pancreatic cancer, which is generally defined as the occurrence of pancreatic cancer in at least one pair of first-degree relatives. Mutations in a gene designated *PALLD* (palladin, or cytoskeletal associated protein) have been linked to familial pancreatic cancer.

ISLET-CELL TUMOURS

Tumours of the endocrine pancreas, which occur in the cells of the islets of Langerhans, are rare and are often classified as functional or nonfunctional tumours. Functional tumours are characterized by excess hormone secretion, whereas nonfunctional tumours, which are more common, do not secrete hormones. The most common functional tumour of the endocrine pancreas is an insulin-secreting tumour called an insulinoma, which is benign in about 90 percent of affected patients. In some cases, hypersecretion of insulin may be caused by diffuse hyperplasia (abnormal increase in cell number) of the islet cells or by a carcinoma (malignant tumour) of the islet cells. A small number of patients with hypersecretion of insulin have islet-cell hyperplasia or single or multiple insulin-secreting tumours (insulinomas) as part of the syndrome known as multiple endocrine neoplasia type 1 (MEN1; characterized primarily by islet, parathyroid, and pituitary tumours). In addition, diffuse hyperplasia of beta cells, called nesidioblastosis, can cause hypoglycemia in infants.

A type of malignant tumour of the endocrine pancreas is the gastrin-secreting tumour called a gastrinoma. The gastrin stimulates the stomach to produce acid, and therefore ulcers of the stomach and duodenum are common. This disorder is known as Zollinger-Ellison syndrome. Gastrinomas may also originate in the stomach and duodenum. Gastrinomas are associated with MEN1 in some patients. A very rare type of tumour of the endocrine pancreas is the glucagon-secreting tumour called a glucagonoma. Glucagonomas cause a "diabetes-dermatitis syndrome" that is characterized by mild diabetes, anemia, and a red blistering rash that appears in one area of the body and then fades, only to reappear at a different site. These patients have very high serum glucagon concentrations but only mild type II diabetes. Other rare tumours of the islet cells include somatostatin-secreting tumours (somatostatinomas) and pancreatic polypeptide-secreting tumours. Tumours of the endocrine pancreas are difficult to diagnose because findings are nonspecific and may include diabetes, gallstones, excessive fat in the stool, indigestion, and diminished secretion of gastric acid. In addition, islet-cell tumours may also produce "ectopic" hormones, meaning that the tumour secretes a hormone that is not normally secreted by the tissue in which the tumour occurs.

DIAGNOSIS AND PROGNOSIS

Blood tests that assess various pancreatic and liver functions may suggest pancreatic cancer. If cancer is suspected, a needle biopsy or an endoscopy procedure is usually conducted to examine pancreatic cells or the pancreas itself for signs of cancer. However, these procedures are invasive and are associated with an increased risk for serious complications, including pancreatitis. In order to make a correct diagnosis and to determine the stage of the cancer, multiple imaging techniques may be employed that allow doctors to see the pancreas despite its location deep within the abdominal cavity. Imaging techniques commonly used include computerized axial tomography (CAT) scans, magnetic resonance imaging (MRI), and different types of ultrasound, including transabdominal ultrasound (imaging performed on the external surface of the abdomen) and endoscopic ultrasound (EUS; an ultrasound device sent through an endoscope to take images of internal tissues). Various techniques that combine contrast agents (dyes) with X-ray imaging are also used to determine whether the bile duct or other ducts within the pancreas are blocked. One example is called percutaneous transhepatic cholangiography (PTC), in which a needle is used to inject a dye directly into the liver, followed by X-ray imaging. Other X-ray imaging techniques include angiography, in which X-rays are used to view blood vessels to determine if the cancer has spread through the walls of the vessels feeding into the pancreas.

Once pancreatic cancer has been diagnosed, its stage is then determined on the basis of how far the cancer has progressed. Stage I cancers are confined to the pancreas and have not spread to nearby lymph nodes. Stage II cancers have spread locally to the bile duct or small intestine but have not reached the lymph nodes, whereas stage III tumours have reached these nodes. Stage IV cancers have spread to other organs such as the lungs, liver, spleen, or colon. The survival rate of persons with pancreatic cancer is lower than that seen with many other cancers because the symptoms of pancreatic cancer often do not become obvious until the later stages of the disease.

TREATMENT AND PREVENTION

When pancreatic cancer is considered to be incurable, major surgery is done mainly to relieve symptoms or digestive problems. Islet-cell tumours are often localized to the tail of the pancreas, and a distal pancreatectomy may be conducted to remove this portion of the pancreas along with the spleen. Exocrine cancers are often treated with the Whipple procedure, a complicated surgical approach that removes all or part of the pancreas and nearby lymph nodes, the gallbladder, and portions of the stomach, small intestine, and bile duct. Other exocrine tumours are sometimes treated by complete removal of the pancreas (total pancreatectomy).

Radiation therapy is sometimes used in conjunction with surgery—often prior to surgery to reduce a tumour

Ken Sheel, suffering with a terminal case of pancreatic cancer, is seen here in his Denver, Colo., home in 2009, embracing his four-year-old son Malakai while a visiting nurse from a nonprofit local hospice looks on. John Moore/Getty Images

to a more manageable size but also after surgery to destroy any remaining cancer cells. The position of the pancreas in the abdominal cavity makes it a difficult target for focused radiotherapy, but a procedure using radiotherapy simultaneously with surgery permits the surgeon to focus radiation directly onto the pancreas by moving obstructing organs aside. Side effects of this radiation therapy may include vomiting, diarrhea, fatigue, and skin irritations resembling a sunburn.

Chemotherapy is generally used when pancreatic cancers have spread to distant organs and may be required so that as many cancer cells as possible can be sought out and destroyed. Endocrine or islet-cell tumours may be treated with hormone therapy, in which specific hormones are used to stop or slow the growth of the cancer in the endocrine cells. Targeted drug therapies that block cellular processes driving cancer-cell proliferation have been used in combination with chemotherapy in some pancreatic cancer patients. For example, a drug called erlotinib (Tarceva) blocks the activity of a kinase (a type of enzyme) associated with the epidermal growth factor receptor (EGFR), which stimulates unregulated cell division when mutated in cancer cells. When erlotinib is given in combination with the chemotherapeutic agent gemcitabine (Gemzar), an antimetabolite that inhibits the synthesis of genetic material in dividing cells, patient survival is improved, although only modestly.

In most cases, pancreatic cancer cannot be completely prevented, but risk can be decreased by reducing or eliminating cigarette smoking and following a diet low in animal products and high in fruits and vegetables. Researchers are also investigating anti-inflammatory therapeutic agents that inhibit an enzyme called cyclooxygenase-2 (COX-2). Because COX-2 plays a role in inflammation and mediates tumour growth and development, it is a valuable target for the development of drugs used in the prevention and treatment of several cancers, including breast cancer, colorectal cancer, and pancreatic cancer. In people at risk for familial pancreatic cancer, routine endoscopy can be used to monitor changes in pancreatic tissue. If tissue abnormalities arise, the pancreas can be removed before cancer develops.

CONCLUSION

The vast number of hormones, the complexity of the endocrine glands, and the large assortment of diseases and disorders of the human endocrine system have long been the subjects of biomedical research. In the past, much of this research was focused on achieving a basic understanding of hormone structure and function and of endocrine disease. Today, while much endocrine research proceeds along these same lines, the questions that scientists seek to answer have grown increasingly complex and in many instances are interrelated, such that discoveries in one area can provide key insights into other areas of research.

Because diabetes mellitus is one of the most common diseases affecting the endocrine system, many researchers are working to better understand the factors that underlie abnormal glucose metabolism. Knowledge of the nuances of the structure and function of insulin has already provided valuable information for the development of new diabetes treatments. However, more work is needed in order to characterize the genes and metabolites that contribute to abnormal glucose metabolism and to insulin resistance and deficiency in particular. For example, studies that analyze genes that mediate sensitivity to insulin could lead to the identification of biomarkers (subtle biochemical changes) that are indicative of diabetes and thereby facilitate the development of new diagnostic and therapeutic approaches.

Other research on the endocrine system has led to surprising discoveries. For example, because the nematode *Caenorhabditis elegans* was discovered to use an insulin signaling pathway nearly identical to the insulin pathway found in human cells, this species has become a valuable model organism for the study of the physiological significance of insulin. Indeed, research on insulin in *C. elegans* has revealed that, in addition to its role in glucose metabolism, the hormone also appears to influence reproduction and aging processes in the nematode. Such findings could have important implications for scientists' understanding of insulin's role in the human body. Similar research on hormones in other model organisms is expected to provide additional intriguing insight into hormones and their diverse functions in the human body.

GLOSSARY

adipose Of or relating to animal fat.

aldosterone A steroid hormone secreted by the adrenal glands.

androgen A male sex hormone (such as testosterone).

arcuate nucleus Any of several cellular masses in the thalamus, hypothalamus, or medulla oblongata.

autocrine Of, relating to, promoted by, or being a substance secreted by a cell and acting on surface receptors of the same cell.

autonomic nervous system In vertebrates, the part of the nervous system that controls and regulates the internal organs without any conscious recognition or effort by the organism.

corpus luteum Yellow, hormone-secreting body in the female reproductive system.

cortisol An organic compound belonging to the steroid family that is the principal hormone secreted by the adrenal glands.

cytokine Any of a group of small, short-lived proteins that are released by one cell to regulate the function of another cell, thereby serving as intercellular chemical messengers.

dopamine A nitrogen-containing organic compound formed as an intermediate compound from dihydroxyphenylalanine (dopa) during the metabolism of the amino acid tyrosine. Dopamine helps control movement. When the amount of this neurotransmitter is low, as happens with Parkinsons disease, a person loses control over the body's movements.

ectopic Occurring in an abnormal position.

electrolyte Any of the ions (as of sodium, potassium, calcium, or bicarbonate) that in a biological fluid regulate or affect most metabolic processes (as the flow of nutrients into and waste products out of cells).

endocrine Producing secretions that are distributed in the body by way of the bloodstream.

endoplasmic reticulum A continuous membrane system that forms a series of flattened sacs within the cytoplasm of a eukaryotic cell and is important in the biosynthesis, processing, and transport of proteins and lipids.

enzyme A substance that acts as a catalyst in living organisms, regulating the rate at which chemical reactions proceed without itself being altered in the process.

exocrine Producing, being, or relating to a secretion that is released outside its source.

exocytosis The release of cellular substances (as secretory products) contained in cell vesicles by fusion of the vesicular membrane with the plasma membrane and subsequent release of the contents to the exterior of the cell.

glucocorticoid Any of a group of corticosteroids (such as cortisol or dexamethasone) that are involved especially in carbohydrate, protein, and fat metabolism.

gonadotropin Any of several hormones occurring in vertebrates that are secreted from the anterior pituitary gland and that act on the gonads (i.e., the ovaries or testes).

homeostasis Any self-regulating process by which biological systems tend to maintain stability while adjusting to conditions that are optimal for survival.

hormone A product of living cells that circulates in body fluids (such as the blood) or sap and produces a specific often stimulatory effect on the activity of cells usually remote from its point of origin.

insulin Hormone that regulates the level of sugar (glucose) in the blood and that is produced by the beta cells of the islets of Langerhans in the pancreas.

leptin A peptide hormone that is produced by fat cells and plays a role in body weight regulation by acting on the hypothalamus to suppress appetite and burn fat stored in adipose tissue.

melatonin Hormone that is derived from serotonin, is secreted by the pineal gland especially in response to darkness, and has been linked to the regulation of circadian rhythms.

metabolite A product of one metabolic process that is essential to another such process in the same organism.

mineralocorticoid A corticoid (as deoxycorticosterone) that affects chiefly the electrolyte and fluid balance in the body.

mitochondrion Any of various round or long cellular organelles of most eukaryotes that are found outside the nucleus, produce energy for the cell through cellular respiration, and are rich in fats, proteins, and enzymes.

neurohemal organ An organ that releases stored neurosecretory substances into the blood.

neurohormone A hormone produced by or acting on nervous tissue.

neurotransmitter A substance (such as norepinephrine or acetylcholine) that transmits nerve impulses across a synapse.

osteoclast Any of the large multinucleate cells closely associated with areas of bone resorption.

oxytocin Hormone that stimulates especially the contraction of uterine muscle and the secretion of milk.

paracrine Of, relating to, promoted by, or being a substance secreted by a cell and acting on adjacent cells.

parathormone Substance produced and secreted by the parathyroid glands that regulates serum calcium concentration.

prolactin A protein hormone of the anterior lobe of the pituitary that induces lactation.

prostaglandin Any of a group of physiologically active substances having diverse hormonelike effects in animals.

proteolytic Of or relating to the hydrolysis of proteins or peptides with formation of simpler and soluble products.

seminiferous tubule Any of the coiled threadlike tubules that make up the bulk of the testis and are lined with a layer of epithelial cells from which the spermatozoa are produced.

senescence The state of being old.

BIBLIOGRAPHY

ENDOCRINOLOGY

Information on the human endocrine system and the diagnosis and treatment of endocrine diseases and disorders is provided in Victor Cornelius, *A History of Endocrinology* (1982); David G. Gardner and Dolores Shoback, *Greenspan's Basic and Clinical Endocrinology*, 8th ed. (2007); Jill B. Becker, et al. (eds.), *Behavioral Endocrinology*, 2nd ed. (2002); Gerald M. Doherty and Britt Skogseid (eds.), *Surgical Endocrinology* (2001); George H. Greeley, Jr. (ed.), *Gastrointestinal Endocrinology* (1999); and Jerome F. Strauss and Robert L. Barbieri (eds.), *Yen and Jaffe's Reproductive Endocrinology: Physiology, Pathophysiology, and Clinical Management*, 5th ed. (2004).

ENDOCRINE GLANDS

Information on specific endocrine glands can be found in Shlomo Melmed (ed.), *The Pituitary*, 2nd ed. (2002); Lewis E. Braverman and Robert D. Utiger (eds.), *Werner's The Thyroid: A Fundamental and Clinical Text*, 9th ed. (2005); and John P. Bilezikian, et al. (eds.), *The Parathyroids: Basic and Clinical Concepts*, 2nd ed. (2001).

DIABETES AND ASSOCIATED CONDITIONS

Diabetes mellitus and related conditions are discussed in *American Diabetes Association Complete Guide to Diabetes*, 4th ed. (2005); O. Paul van Bijsterveld (ed.), *Diabetic*

Retinopathy (2000); Aubie Angel, et al. (eds.), *Diabetes and Cardiovascular Disease: Etiology, Treatment, and Outcomes* (2001); Aristidis Veves (ed.), *Clinical Management of Diabetic Neuropathy* (1998); and Ronald G. Gill, et al. (eds.), *Immunologically Mediated Endocrine Diseases* (2002).

HORMONES

Comprehensive works on the biochemistry of the hormones of the endocrine system include Albert L. Lehninger, David L. Nelson, and Michael L. Cox, *Lehninger Principles of Biochemistry*, 5th ed. (2008); Thomas Briggs and Albert M. Chandler (eds.), *Biochemistry*, 3rd ed. (1995); and John W. Hill, Dorothy M. Feigl, and Stuart J. Baum, *Chemistry and Life: An Introduction to General, Organic, and Biological Chemistry*, 5th ed. (1997). David J. Holme and Hazel Peck, *Analytical Biochemistry*, 3rd ed. (1998), covers methods of analysis. A specific reference on neurohormones is Richard E. Brown, *An Introduction to Neuroendocrinology* (2002).

INDEX

"fight-or-flight" response,
  15, 65
follicle-stimulating hormone
  (FSH), 20, 38–41, 65, 66, 68,
  82, 83, 88, 90, 91, 93, 94, 112,
  113, 118, 128
Fröhlich, Alfred, 169
Fröhlich syndrome, 169–170

G

gastric-inhibitory polypeptide, 70
gastrin, 52, 68, 69, 70, 121
gastrointestinal neuropeptides, 68
ghrelin, 44
gigantism/pituitary gigantism,
  45, 173, 174, 175–176, 177
glucagon, 15, 22, 52, 58, 68, 69, 81,
  120, 180
glucagon tolerance test, 58
glucocorticoids, 21, 33, 36, 37,
  72–73, 135, 136, 159, 162,
  163, 164
glucose tolerance test, 58–60, 186
goitre, 1, 113, 132–134, 135, 137, 138,
  139, 141, 142, 147
gonadotropin-releasing hormone
  (GnRH), 24, 41–42, 68, 70,
  82, 88, 93, 113
gonadotropins, 16, 24, 26, 38–41,
  41–42, 70, 82, 88, 90, 105, 112,
  113, 129, 146, 169, 177
gonads, 9, 16, 20, 29, 38, 42, 103,
  105, 106, 110, 115, 116
  ovaries, 3, 9, 20, 38, 39, 41, 42,
  46, 63, 64, 72, 81–84, 107,
  110, 115, 127, 128, 139, 146, 177
  testes, 2, 3, 9, 20, 38, 39, 41, 63,
  64, 72, 92–94, 110, 111, 112,
  113, 114, 115, 177

granulomatous thyroiditis,
  134–135, 139
Graves, Robert, 138
Graves disease, 62, 126, 134,
  135–136, 138, 141, 147
growth and differentiation/
  development, control of, 12,
  14–15, 30–31, 43, 44, 45
growth factors, 11
growth hormone, 11, 19, 23, 26,
  30, 31, 32, 42–43, 44, 45, 51,
  66, 67, 68, 70, 78, 81, 90, 105,
  116, 117, 120, 121, 127, 129,
  146, 170–172, 177, 178
growth hormone deficiency,
  170–172
growth hormone excess,
  172–176
growth hormone-releasing
  hormone (GHRH), 43–44,
  67, 78, 171, 173

H

Hashimoto disease, 62,
  137–138, 142
hepatic portal circulation, 22
hermaphroditism, 109–111
homeostasis, maintenance of,
  12–14
hormone-receptor complex, 6
hormones
  how they work, 6
  synthesis of, 18–21, 32
  transport of, 18, 22–23, 32
human chorionic gonadotropin
  (HCG), 39, 118, 179
Hunter, John, 2
hyperaldosteronism, 160,
  165–167

hypercalcemia, 35, 85, 117, 118,
151–153, 154
hypercalcitoninemia, 138, 146
hyperglycemia, 180–181, 183, 185,
186, 187
hyperkalemia, 74, 159, 167
hyperparathyroidism, 51, 120,
121, 122, 124, 150–153,
hyperthyroidism, 61, 62, 100, 118,
132, 135, 136, 138–141, 142,
147, 177
hypoaldosteronism, 167–168
hypocalcemia, 85, 146, 153, 154
hypoglycemia, 117, 118, 180,
181–183, 189, 190
hypogonadism, 42, 111–113, 115,
126, 128
hyponatremia, 117, 118, 130,
159, 167
hypoparathyroidism, 51, 150,
153–154
hypopituitarism, 148,
170, 176
hypothalamic-hypophyseal
portal circulation, 22
hypothalamic-pituitary-target
gland axis, 9, 10, 29
hypothalamus, 9, 10, 16, 22, 24,
25, 33, 35, 41, 42, 44, 46, 47,
51, 53, 54, 56, 67–68, 70, 73,
74–75, 77, 78, 82, 88, 89, 91,
92, 93, 100, 111, 174
anatomy of, 75
diseases and disorders of, 111,
112, 113, 144, 155, 158, 159, 162,
168–170, 176, 178
regulation of hormone
secretion, 75–78
hypothyroidism, 54, 60–61, 100,

106, 126, 132, 137, 138, 139,
142–145, 146, 148

I

inhibin, 39, 65, 94
insulin, 14, 19, 22, 24, 43, 44, 52,
68, 69, 70, 80–81, 107, 118,
120, 131, 163, 180, 181, 182,
183, 185, 186, 188–190, 191,
192, 197–198
insulin-like growth factors
(IGFs), 23, 43, 44–45, 70,
118, 127, 129, 172
integrative functions, 12,
16–17

J

Jacobs, Patricia A., 114
jet lag, 26–29

K

Kallmann syndrome, 42
Klinefelter, Harry, 114
Klinefelter syndrome, 109, 112,
113–115

L

lactotrophs, 19
Langerhans, islets of, 3, 15, 19, 22,
29, 52, 63, 68, 80–81, 120, 173,
182, 183, 185, 189, 192
Langerhans, Paul, 80
Laron dwarfism, 172
Lerner, Aaron B., 46
limbic system, 42